LIGHTROOM
TRANSFORMATIONS

REALIZING YOUR VISION WITH LIGHTROOM—PLUS PHOTOSHOP

MARTIN EVENING

New Riders | VOICES THAT MATTER™

Lightroom Transformations:
Realizing your vision with Adobe Lightroom—plus Photoshop
Martin Evening

New Riders
www.newriders.com

To report errors, please send a note to errata@peachpit.com
New Riders is an imprint of Peachpit, a division of Pearson Education.

Acquisitions Editor: Valerie Witte
Developmental and Copy Editor: Peggy Nauts
Production Editor: Tracey Croom
Proofreader: Patricia J. Pane
Composition: Martin Evening
Indexer: James Minkin
Cover Design: Mimi Heft
Interior Design: Mimi Heft, with Martin Evening
Cover Image: Martin Evening

ISBN-13: 9780134398280
ISBN-10: 0134398289

9 8 7 6 5 4 3 2 1
Printed and bound in the United States of America

INTRODUCTION

My first encounter with digital imaging was in the late '80s, when I had one of my photographs retouched by a Quantel Paintbox system operator. I was instantly hooked. A few years later, with the arrival of Photoshop, it became possible to retouch photographs on a home computer, and I remember telling my partner at the time that I really needed to get my own Photoshop system. "And what exactly do you need this Photoshop thing for?" she asked. It was a good question. Why exactly did I need Photoshop? Very few photographers I knew of were using it. None of my clients were requesting digital image manipulation. Occasionally on advertising jobs, photographs were retouched digitally, but this was always carried out by an agency-sourced operator and never the photographers themselves.

Even so, after a few years I had saved up enough money to acquire my first image-editing workstation running Photoshop. Once I had gotten over the usual excitement of swapping heads and skies and playing with the special effects filters, I settled down to a serious study of how to use Photoshop, and later Lightroom, as a digital darkroom tool. These days, you'd be hard put to find a professional photographer who never uses image-editing software. The type of Photoshop and Lightroom editing work I do now with my own photographs leans more toward an understated style of retouching, and it is not obvious that the photographs have been manipulated. For me, it is more about knowing how to configure the camera settings to capture the best possible raw file and then understanding how to best use the tools in Lightroom and Photoshop to perfect the image. In this book I share these skills and show how you can unleash the full potential of your photographs.

ACKNOWLEDGMENTS

I would like to thank my acquisitions editor, Valerie Witte, who did a fabulous job guiding me through this project from the early planning to the final proof stages. Many thanks to my developmental and copy editor, Peggy Nauts; proofreader, Patricia J. Pane; and project editor, Tracey Croom, who all helped me look good. And thank you also to Mimi Heft for the design work and to James Minkin, who did the indexing.

I am grateful to the following photographers, who allowed me to use their photographs in the book: Ansell Cizic, Angela Di Martino, Chris Ducker, Chris Evans, Richard Eyers, Guy Pilkington, Eric Richmond, and Farid Sani. And I also wish to thank key members of the Lightroom team: Joshua Bury, Kelly Castro, Eric Chan, Tom Hogarty, Thomas Knoll, Max Wendt, Simon Chen, Julie Kmoch, Julieanne Kost, Sharad Mangalick, Becky Sowada, Jeff Tranberry, Benjamin Warde, and Ben Zibble.

Lastly, I would like to thank my wife, Camilla, and daughter, Angelica, for their patience while I was busy researching and writing this book.

DOWNLOADING BONUS MATERIALS

To accompany the book, I have produced a number of tutorial videos that will allow you to follow the steps used to transform the images featured in this book.

To access and download the bonus content:

1. Visit peachpit.com/register.

2. Log in with your Peachpit account, or if you don't have one, create an account.

3. Register using the book's ISBN, 9780134398280. This title will then appear in the Registered Products area of your account, and you can click the Access Bonus Content link to be taken to the page where you can view the videos.

CONTENTS

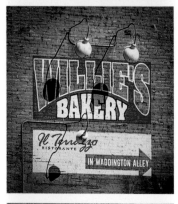

1

WHAT MAKES A GOOD PHOTOGRAPH?

POINTS TO CONSIDER BEFORE YOU SHOOT

WHAT ARE YOU TRYING TO SAY?

It may seem like an obvious question, but what are you trying to say with your photography? Photographs can be used in all kinds of ways: as an art form, to educate, illustrate, sell things, or simply record personal moments. Whatever you photograph, there has to be a reason or purpose to your photography if it is to have any meaning. Photographing to please yourself is fine if the aim is simply to enjoy your photography and create pretty pictures, but you can improve your photography by making an honest self-appraisal of what your aims are and whether you are meeting them or not. With commercial photography, the photographs you take will need to meet the needs of the client rather than fulfill your own desires. You will be expected to record a scene or event, illustrate a product at its best, or sell a concept. Photographing for clients is demanding and taxing, but it's also a great way to improve your photography, because it makes you think more carefully about the message you are trying to convey with the goal of satisfying your client. However, many students tend to shoot whatever interests them, and the focus or discipline isn't always there. If you shoot professionally and your photographs don't communicate what your clients want, they will soon let you know.

For the past 15 years I have written a regular column for What Digital Camera and more recently, Amateur Photographer magazine, in which I review readers' images and show how they can be improved. When I first started writing these columns, digital photography was only just starting to become popular. Consequently, a lot of the submitted photos were scanned images or shot on primitive digital

THE VIEWING PUBLIC
IS VISUALLY LITERATE
ENOUGH TO DISTINGUISH
BETWEEN NEWS-REPORTING
IMAGES, WHICH SHOULD
BE FACTUAL AND HONEST,
AND ADVERTISING AND
MAGAZINE PHOTOS THAT
DISTORT REALITY.

cameras. As the technical quality of the cameras has improved, the quality of the photographs submitted has noticeably improved, too. Even so, I find a lot of photographers are not making the best use of the tone and color software controls that are available to them. This book is about learning how to master the Develop controls in Lightroom and how and when to enlist Photoshop to make the most of the image data in the capture image.

I have a Canadian cousin, Marek Forysinski (who is featured later in this book), who works as a musician, producer, and sound engineer. When he works with music artists, his role is to take multitrack recordings and craft something special from the raw talent. In many ways this is how I see my job, whether I am working with my own photographs or editing and critiquing a reader's photograph for a magazine article.

Often I hear photographers proudly boast that they didn't do anything to edit their photographs, implying that those that have been touched by a computer are somehow less pure. The thing is, if you shoot in JPEG mode you are letting the camera's onboard processor make all the editing decisions for you, and the downside of this is that further editing options become more limited (which is why it is better to shoot raw). But whether you shoot JPEG or raw, this is still only the starting point to produce something better. Some people question whether it is legitimate to retouch images digitally, but there is really nothing new about using Lightroom or Photoshop to edit your photographs rather than working in a darkroom. All that's different is the extent to which you can edit. So the question should really be not whether it is OK to retouch or not, but how much reworking is acceptable?

The answer mainly depends on how the photographs are going to be used. Among photojournalists, legitimate concerns have been raised about unscrupulous retouching and what is permissible. Most news photographers take the view that it is OK to do things like crop, fine-tune the tone and color, and selectively darken or lighten for emphasis. What's not OK is to use cloning methods to remove or add anything, beyond getting rid of dust sensor marks. Meanwhile, in the world of advertising, the photography and retouching are very clever and, quite clearly, artificial. I don't think there is anything dishonest about this approach unless the result is seriously misleading or breaks advertising guidelines. Overall, the viewing public is visually literate enough to distinguish between news-reporting images, which should be factual and honest, and advertising and magazine photos that distort reality.

My career using Photoshop began over 20 years ago, when I got my first computer and installed Photoshop 2.5. I have therefore witnessed the development and use of Photoshop, and then Lightroom, from an early stage and seen how these two programs have influenced the way photographers process their pictures. Much of the commercial work I have produced has involved combining studio photography with Photoshop retouching. It's paid the bills and helped me build a separate career as an author, but at heart I prefer the simpler approaches to image editing. There are some great Photoshop artists out there, such as Bert Monroy and Erik Johansson, who produce amazing Photoshop compositions, but my personal preference is to use Lightroom and Photoshop as little as possible. It sounds easy, and it is once you understand how to capture the optimum image detail at the shooting stage and how to then fine-tune the appearance of your photographs using Lightroom and Photoshop in a subtle manner.

ESSENTIAL STEPS FOR OPTIMUM QUALITY

At the very minimum you should aim to capture your photographs using the lowest recommended ISO setting with the optimum shutter speed and aperture setting for the subject matter you are photographing, which in turn will be dependent on the lens you are using and the pixel density of the sensor. I cover these topics in more detail in the following chapter. Other than that you need to make sure the image is sharp where it needs to be in focus. When you shoot in raw mode, everything else such as the white balance, tone adjustments, color profile, noise reduction, and sharpening can be taken care of later in the postprocessing. These are the key steps to obtaining technical perfection.

FRAMING THE IMAGE

While the lens aperture, shutter speed, and focus have to be right at the capture stage, it is also important you frame the subject correctly. What matters most is your choice of viewpoint, coupled with the choice of lens to determine the angle of view. In any given situation there are usually several good viewpoints and hundreds of bad ones. It's hard to say what the best angle is for all cases, but here are a few tips and suggestions.

The key areas of interest need to be clearly visible

To make sure your subject or subjects stand out clearly, you usually have to get close to your subject, or use a longer lens so that the subject fills the frame more. Beginners tend to make the mistake of standing too far back and then wondering why their friends look so small in their photographs. You want to ensure distracting elements that might confuse the viewer are kept to a minimum. This is where the choice of angle is critical, and it is important to explore different viewpoints. If you are going to shoot on location, you can use a map to plan where the optimum viewing angle might be and how the elements in a landscape might line up. Once there, the first thing you need to do is explore all available angles before you set up the tripod. In the studio, you should always consider the position of the camera first before you set up the lighting. Again, I always hand-hold the camera first and explore all possible angles before it goes anywhere near a tripod.

WHEN YOU SHOOT IN RAW MODE, EVERYTHING ELSE SUCH AS THE WHITE BALANCE, TONE ADJUSTMENTS, COLOR PROFILE, NOISE REDUCTION, AND SHARPENING CAN BE TAKEN CARE OF LATER.

Lead the eye into the frame

Look for visual elements that help lead the eye into the picture or balance the composition better by filling busy or empty spaces. For example, shooting from a low angle can allow you to de-emphasize a distracting foreground or background. Also, by shooting from low down, close-up objects can be made to appear taller and fill the frame more. You can also use elements in a scene to lead the viewer's eye. Photographer Tim Flach has some interesting ideas about how the composition in paintings and photographs determines how we read them. He has observed how classical painters would often use visual tricks to lead the eye in from the left in a sweeping direction to the center of the picture. The methods used can be quite subtle.

Figure 1.1 shows one of my own photographs, where you can see there are several points of entry coming from the left that lead the eye into the tree in the middle. I wouldn't claim there was any conscious calculation to photograph this way. I happened to be in a park at the right time with the right lighting when a young boy was cycling along the route of the maze. I took a number of photographs of this scene but selected this one because I liked it more than the others. It is only when you analyze these subconscious decisions later that you realize why some compositions stand out more than others and how the capture decisions you make become instinctive the more you photograph.

FIGURE 1.1 In this image, several entry points lead the eye in from the left to the center of the frame, marked on the above photograph.

Look for shapes within the frame

In any given situation, there will be key elements you want to emphasize in the shot. Apart from the main subject, there are likely to be other objects that you may want to include, or within a specific location there may be certain angles that work better than others because a particular arrangement gives the image a better balance. In any given situation, you will want to look for the optimum angle. Look for elements that act as a frame within a frame, such as a leaning tree or a door frame. These are obvious examples, but there are also more subtle ways you can frame an image, such as through the use of light and shade. In Chapter 5, I have included a number of examples where I was able to adjust the positioning of the elements in the original capture to produce a stronger composition.

Lighting

The lighting is extremely important. Lighting can be used to direct the eye to play up or play down certain areas. When shooting on location, the time of day and weather can make a big difference. Locations can change dramatically in appearance and are usually at their best when photographed with early morning, late evening, or overcast light. With other types of subjects, studio lights can be used to add emphasis where it is needed and mask those areas that are best hidden. In the days of color transparency film, the lighting at the capture stage was supercritical, as you only had one chance to get everything right. With black-and-white and color negative film, there was more flexibility at the print-making stage to dodge and burn to refine the lighting. Whether you shot using transparency or negative, the ideal way to light was to ensure there was always a background fill of some kind to fill the shadows and use the main lights to provide the light shaping. This practice is still applicable today when you shoot digitally, because having a base fill light gives you the option to pull out or suppress the shadow detail as desired.

Perspective

The image that's focused on the sensor is an abstract representation of reality. The challenge for camera lens designers has been to work out how to bend the rays of light entering the lens so that the image appears in sharp focus from the center to the edges of the sensor. At the same time, the lens optics in rectilinear lenses have been designed to produce an image in which straight lines in a scene are mapped as straight lines in the image. This can also be helped through the application of lens profile corrections in Lightroom's Camera Raw. Although it is pleasing to see lines kept straight and circles prevented from becoming elliptical, these are all a distortion of reality. While a fisheye lens view may look distorted, it is probably closer to how a scene is perceived by our eyes as we scan what is around us. It is our brain, which processes what we observe, that sees straight lines as actually being straight. However

WHILE A FISHEYE LENS VIEW MAY LOOK DISTORTED, IT IS PROBABLY CLOSER TO HOW A SCENE IS PERCEIVED BY OUR EYES AS WE SCAN WHAT IS AROUND US.

you choose to create a 2D image to represent a 3D scene, you are manipulating the perspective in some way (see **Figure 1.2**). Landscape artists have always played fast and loose with the rules of perspective, and there is no reason why you can't do that, too. Later, in Chapter 6, I show how the Adaptive Wide Angle filter can be used to selectively manipulate the perspective in an image.

FIGURE 1.2 The scene was photographed (top left) using a full-frame fisheye lens, uncorrected so you can see the curvature distortion. You can process an image captured in this way to produce a rectilinear projection (top right), which in turn was captured from the 360° panorama stitch view (bottom).

Break the rules

You can, of course, disregard the classic rules of composition and follow your own intuition, just as it's perfectly OK to lose detail in the shadows or highlights, shoot portraits with an extreme wide-angle lens, or take photographs outdoors when the sun is high in the sky or when it is raining. There don't have to be any constraints on what you do. The rules are simply guidelines; if you can achieve something greater by breaking them, kudos to you.

IMAGE SELECTIONS AND RATING

IT IS BEST TO BE SPARING WITH THE HIGHER STAR RATINGS. FOUR- AND FIVE-STAR RATINGS SHOULD BE RESERVED FOR ONLY THE FINEST PORTFOLIO-QUALITY PHOTOGRAPHS.

After you have taken your photographs, it is important to know how to identify the best shots. Photographers typically end up shooting hundreds of photographs every week. It's therefore all too easy to lose track of your best shots if you don't take the time to edit them properly. Lightroom is ideal for this task. As soon as you import your photographs, you can use the keypad to rate your photos using 0–5 stars as you review them. It is best to do this as close as possible to the time you took the shots. My system is to leave the reject shots as being unrated with a zero star and rate the shots of interest with a one-star rating. Having done that, I make a filtered selection of the one-star images and apply two stars to the ones that are best in that selection. In some instances I'll carry out a further edit to apply three-star ratings, but I tend not to give any photo four or five stars at this stage because I feel it is best to be sparing with the higher star ratings. Four- and five-star ratings should be reserved for only the finest portfolio-quality photographs.

It is usually best to allow time for the initial previews to render. If you are going to make subjective judgments about the quality of what you have shot, you need to approve shots in some kind of optimized state. As you will see throughout this book, a lot of images don't necessarily look that interesting with just the default develop settings applied. If you have shot a series of pictures in the same location, you might want to process the first image and sync the settings with the rest, wait for those to render, and then carry out a review edit to apply the star ratings. Or, you might want to configure Lightroom to apply Auto Tone settings by default.

Finding a fresh perspective

It's not always easy to sort out the hero shots from the rest in one go. I find it helps to step away from the reviewing process and edit the photos again the following day. Most of us tend to concentrate on specific things when we look at our photographs. For example, on a fashion shoot I find that the clothes stylist will zone in on the clothes, the hairdresser the hair, and the model will check how good she is looking. As for the photographer, she may just be looking at the lighting and composition, whereas in fact, she should be looking at everything that's going on in the photos. Beginner photographers tend to see past the imperfections and visualize the image in a slightly different way from the rest of us. It's therefore important to train yourself to view your photos as others see them. That is also why it helps to have others critique your work.

To illustrate this point, some years ago I was approached by an art director at AMV BBDO agency in London to help work on an advertising competition. The theme was protecting the environment, and the art director came up with the concept of 'What would it be like to be a fish trying to breathe in polluted water?' The idea he had was of a man suffocated by a plastic bag. Having discussed the brief, I enlisted the help of a friend of mine, Martin Soan, who was a comedy performer, and we arranged to do the shoot later that day. I got hold of a few plastic bags and used a spare room in my flat as a makeshift studio. I bounced a couple of tungsten lights off the walls and ceiling so as to get some nice reflections on the plastic. The photos were taken with a medium-format film camera using a 140 mm lens at the widest aperture so there was a nice, shallow focus.

FIGURE 1.3 One of the contact sheets for the "acid rain" shoot.

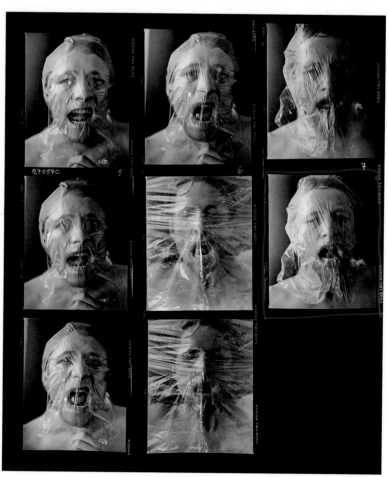

FIGURE 1.4 The final image used for the advertising competition. We needed to show what it would be like to be a fish trying to breathe in water that had been polluted by acid rain.

It was Martin Soan who came up with the idea of using a sheet of cling film instead of a regular plastic bag and who provided us with some suitably startled expressions. In **Figure 1.3**, you can see one of the contact sheets from the shoot. The next day I showed these to the art director, and together we made a short-list selection of photos, where we picked out the wilder expressions, such as those in the left strip in Figure 1.3. A few hours later I got a call saying the agency's creative director, Alfredo Marcantonio, had spotted a photo where Martin didn't look so posed. Out of all the rolls of film that had been shot, it was the only one where Martin looked as if he really was about to faint (see **Figure 1.4**). On reflection, this was definitely the best shot from the session, and the art director and I had missed it and were both grateful for someone else's fresh perspective.

WHAT'S THE STORY?

To return to my original theme, what is it you are trying to say? For a photograph to have any meaning, it should be more than an end in itself. It is all very well creating a picture that is technically perfect, but unless it conveys some kind of message, what is the point? For the last 15 years I have probably analyzed hundreds of photographs sent in by amateur photographer readers. The good ones have been those pictures that tell a story or show a fresh perspective. I have also been able to demonstrate that within every good shot there is nearly always the potential to create something better. Even if the viewpoint isn't always perfect, or the composition is a bit confused, there are lots of things you can do at the postprocessing stage that mimic what was traditionally done in the darkroom to bring such photos to life and make them shine. Several examples in this book prove that it took only a few slider adjustments to get the finished look, which is why it is important to fully understand what those sliders do and when it is appropriate to apply them. Also, we'll cover when it is appropriate to work in Lightroom and when it is best to use Photoshop.

That, in a nutshell, is what this book is all about. I want to teach you how to work out which elements in your photographs are the most important and how to make these stand out. It is admittedly a more restrained approach to the use of Lightroom and Photoshop than some photographers employ, but one that can transform your photography immeasurably.

2

OPTIMIZE

GETTING THE BEST FROM YOUR CAMERA CAPTURES

FROM CAMERA TO PRINT

To obtain the best results, you obviously need to invest in the best camera equipment and lenses, but you also need to learn how to use them effectively and avoid the bad habits that can have a detrimental effect on the image quality. This chapter is mainly about the things you can do at the capture stage to obtain the sharpest images, plus how you can use the Develop controls in Lightroom to optimize the sharpness, noise reduction, tone, and color output. I also explain the ideal workflow for moving images from Lightroom to Photoshop and back again, followed by how to optimize your images for print using the Print module in Lightroom.

The main objective here is for you to devise a safe workflow in which the steps you apply in Lightroom and Photoshop cause the least amount of harm as you take a raw photo through the various steps from the camera sensor capture to the print-output stage. None of these steps are particularly complicated, and a lot can easily be automated so that each time you import files into Lightroom, the program automatically applies the necessary lens corrections and color profile settings. You can even configure Lightroom to automatically apply varying degrees of noise reduction according to the ISO speed the files were shot with. When it comes to the print stage, a lot of steps need to be configured correctly within Lightroom as well as at the system level. But here, too, it is possible to record all of these within a single preset to keep the printing foolproof and consistent.

The instructions in this chapter have deliberately been kept as simple as possible. I have provided lots of examples of best-practice guidelines as well as the logic behind these recommendations so readers can have a clear understanding of what the issues are and how best to resolve them.

LENS APERTURE AND SHUTTER SPEED SELECTION

FACTORS AFFECTING LENS SHARPNESS

For optimum image quality, you want the best optics you can afford. That's logical enough, but how you use the lens is just as important. And as sensor megapixel counts have increased, it is critical that you get this right. To do justice to a high-resolution pixel sensor, you need a lens that can resolve detail to the point where those extra pixels can be truly appreciated. Generally speaking, prime lenses are better than zoom lenses because they have fewer glass elements and are optimized for a fixed focal length. But having said that, some of the latest zoom lenses do now offer exceptional sharpness that can match or supersede some prime lenses. Of course, such zooms are more expensive. If you are interested in comparing optical performance, the Dxomark.com website contains a database of most current lenses for digital SLRs (dSLRs), where you can check out its lens evaluation results.

The transmission quality is linked to the maximum lens aperture a lens can shoot at. The wider the aperture, or lower the f-stop number, the brighter the lens. When using an f/1.2 lens, the view seen through the viewfinder of an SLR camera at maximum aperture will be almost as bright as in normal viewing. The benefit of using such lenses is that shooting at a wide aperture produces a shallow focus, which can give your photographs a large-format feel.

Most lenses perform at their best when stopped down to somewhere between f/8 and f/16. The "sweet spot" will vary with individual lenses. At the widest aperture the image will be acceptably sharp in the center but less so at the edges, and the depth of field will be shallowest, which means getting the focus right is critical. As you stop down midway, you will see more even sharpness from the center to the edges and the lens will be at its sharpest setting overall. The depth of field will also increase, creating the perception that more elements are in focus around the point of sharpest focus. As you stop down to the smallest aperture setting, the lens sharpness will deteriorate. This is due to light diffraction caused by the small aperture, which softens the contrast so the image appears to be less sharp. It is a bit like what happens when you squint your eyes as you look at something.

On the other hand, shooting at the smallest aperture increases the depth of field—sometimes it can be more important to obtain a greater depth of field so that more things appear to be in sharp focus. There is also a school of thought that when shooting with the latest high-resolution sensors, while the sharpness appearance may be diminished at the smallest apertures, an image shot at, say, f/16 or f/22 can be sharpened more at the postprocessing stage to produce a result that looks as sharp as if shot at f/8. Because of the increased depth of field, a more aggressive approach to the sharpening is less prone to generating ugly artifacts, because nearly everything in the image will be in focus.

If you shoot with the camera hand-held, the slowest shutter speed you should use is dependent to some extent on the focal length of the lens you are shooting with. An old rule of thumb is that the shutter speed you select should not be less than the focal length of the lens. So, if you were to shoot using a 50 mm lens, you would not want to shoot with a shutter speed any less than 1/50th. As you increase the focal length of the lens, any camera movement will become accentuated; hence the need for faster shutter speeds. However, now that sensors have much higher pixel resolutions, that rule needs to be revised so that you will need to at least double the shutter speed. In other words, if shooting with a 50 mm lens, you should aim to shoot using at least 1/100th of a second.

The way you hold the camera is important, too. With a dSLR type camera, you normally hold the camera up to your eye and can balance your elbows against your body for extra support. With a mirrorless camera, the photographers may shoot by holding it in midair so they can view the image on the rear screen. This is a bad idea because you can't really keep the camera steady. Other mirrorless cameras feature a rangefinder or electronic viewfinder, so you can hold the camera closer to your body as you would using a dSLR.

Some lenses and camera systems include image stabilization, which can either be done via the lens or the camera itself by moving the sensor. The latter method means such cameras can work with any lens rather than just those with built-in image stabilization. In practice the technology works well and can give you an extra couple of stops by allowing you to shoot hand-held at what would normally be considered less than ideal shutter speeds. Image stabilizing is most useful when working with long focus lenses where you need the freedom to follow fast-moving subjects and gain extra speed to freeze the action (see **Figure 2.1**). Modern image-stabilizing systems work really well, though I prefer to make sure the image stabilization is switched off when shooting with the camera mounted on a tripod, especially if making a long time exposure.

If you shoot using a tripod, you have the freedom to select slower shutter speeds, unless the subject you are photographing is moving, of course. In these situations you might like to consider making use of the mirror-up facility on dSLR cameras. When it's enabled, you press the shutter once to flip the mirror up and then again to fire the shutter. The benefit of doing this is it removes the vibrations caused immediately after the mirror flips up. Basically, when you hand-hold a camera and shoot, your hand acts as a dampener that absorbs the vibration. When the camera is fixed on a tripod, it is more prone to the effect of such vibrations because there is nothing to cushion it. I have found the problem is most noticeable at a shutter speed of 1/60th of a second. At slower speeds, the shutter is open long enough that the length of the vibration is

FIGURE 2.1 This photograph was captured using a 70–200 mm zoom lens with image stabilization enabled to help freeze the action at a shutter speed of 1/1000 of a second. I also had to pan the camera to follow the action to ensure the subject remained sharp.

limited relative to the length of the total exposure. At faster shutter speeds, the briefness of the exposure time is sufficient to overcome the problem of vibration. Enabling mirror-up mode is a wise precaution whenever possible and essential if shooting at shutter speeds close to 1/60th, even more so if using a high-pixel-resolution sensor.

A screw-on UV lens can protect the lens surface from getting scratched and prevent dust from getting in. However, even if a UV filter is high quality, it can have an adverse effect on the image quality. This is most noticeable with wide-angle lenses. With long focus lenses, the angle of view is more or less perpendicular to the filter glass. But with a wide-angle lens the angle of view toward the edges means light is coming in at an angle through the glass and is therefore refracted more than light coming straight through the central axis at a perpendicular angle. If you are going to use UV filters only, fit them to your longer lenses. Whenever you are shooting with a filter in front of the lens, make sure the glass is kept clean and free of dust, and also be careful when shooting into the sun, because whenever you have a filter placed in front of the lens, it can make the lens flare worse.

While it is obviously a good idea to ensure the lens elements remain scratch-free, small scratches won't impair the optical lens performance so much compared with things like smear marks or lens flare. For instance, the glass that covers the lens on your smartphone is unprotected and subject to a lot of rough treatment but is still capable of capturing amazingly sharp images. But if you allow the glass covering the lens to get smeared, your images will have a very noticeable soft-focus look.

A lot of photographers like to rely on autofocus, which can work well providing the lenses you shoot with are correctly calibrated for the camera you are using. Small fluctuations in the camera and lens assembly can significantly affect the reliability of the autofocusing. So if your shots aren't looking as sharp as you'd like them to be when autofocus is enabled, it might come down to the lenses being miscalibrated. Not all cameras allow you to do this, but on professional dSLRs you should find there is a custom menu item that will allow you to compensate for any misalignment in the autofocus system. You can do this for each individual lens you shoot with. Once you have done that, the camera will know just how much to compensate the autofocus setting when a particular lens is attached and focus more accurately. You can calibrate by setting up the camera to photograph a sheet of newsprint, or you can use something like the Lens Align system (Michaeltapesdesign.com), which has been especially designed to help make it easier to detect whether your camera is autofocusing too close or too far away from the measured point of focus.

Autofocus is great for those times when you need to shoot quickly and don't have time to check the focus or you need assistance tracking a moving subject. For all other situations, I prefer to focus manually, which can also be done using the live view function on the camera and then zooming in on the live view preview to the maximum zoom setting and checking the focus. The only thing to watch out for is that excessive use of the live view can soon drain the camera battery, so make sure you carry enough spares when you shoot on location.

FIXING CAMERA SHAKE IN PHOTOSHOP

You'll want to avoid camera shake where possible. You can do this by opening up the lens aperture or increasing the ISO setting so you can increase the shutter speed. Or, find a way to stabilize the camera. Failing that, it is now possible to remove camera shake using the Shake Reduction filter in Photoshop. To be honest, this filter has never really lived up to the excitement generated by the demo first shown at Adobe Max in 2011, and it has been hard to find examples of where the filter can actually do a great job. That was until I saw the photograph shown here, which was shot by Chris Ducker. This photograph was taken early one morning, and because of the low light it had to be shot hand-held at a shutter speed of 1/20th of a second. Even when taking a photograph with a wide-angle lens, this is pushing the limits for a hand-held shot without the use of some form of image stabilization. The following steps show how I was able to fix this using the Shake Reduction filter.

1 I opened the image in Photoshop, where I went to the Filter menu and chose Sharpen ⇨ Shake Reduction. There are a number of options to play with in this filter dialog, but more often than not the default shake reduction will be just the right amount to apply. The Shake Reduction filter works by examining the image in detail and estimating the blur trace angle for the camera movement. Once this is known, the filter uses a deconvolution process to undo the camera shake and make the photograph appear sharper.

2 Here you can see the final image. The close-up views below show how the image looked before and after the Shake Reduction filter was applied. If you look closely, there are some sharpening artifacts, but the filtered version is still a big improvement.

No shake reduction

With shake reduction applied

Photograph: © Chris Ducker

LENS CORRECTIONS

You can address a lack of sharpness by adding sharpening at the postprocessing stage, but this is only effective to a certain degree and is no substitute for shooting with better optics in the first place. Other lens artifacts include geometric distortion, where pincushion or barrel distortion causes straight lines in an image to appear curved. Lens vignetting is where the exposure drops off toward the edge of the picture, causing the corners of the frame to appear darker. Lastly, lenses can suffer from chromatic aberration.

Lateral chromatic aberration results in color fringes being seen around sharp edges toward the edges of the frame. This is most noticeable with wide-angle lenses because the image created at the periphery of the frame is from light that has traveled through the lens elements at a more extreme angle compared with light focusing an image at the center. Consequently, light is refracted more so that the different wavelengths of light are focused at slightly separate points. Think, for example, about the way a triangular prism can be used to split a white beam of light into a rainbow spectrum. When you shot using a film camera, the color film contained three color-sensitive emulsions laid directly on top of each other. The effects of lateral chromatic aberration were there but more diffuse. With digital cameras, the effects are more noticeable because of the arrangement of the photosites on a camera sensor and the fact that the image is recorded as three distinct color channels of red, green, and blue. Although this makes the lateral chromatic aberration more obvious, it is also easier to fix in postprocessing. Such images can be corrected by rescaling the individual color channels so they are all in register at the outer edges.

Axial chromatic aberration can occur where different wavelengths of light are focused at different points in front as well as behind the point of sharpest focus. This can occur at any point of the image and not just at the edges and is most noticeable when shooting at the widest lens apertures. This type of chromatic aberration can also be caused by ghosting or charge leakage (something that affects older CCD sensors). These will typically appear purple or magenta when they're in front of the plane of focus and green when they're behind the plane of focus. But even at the exact point of focus, you may sometimes see purple fringes (especially along high contrast or backlit edges), which can be caused by lens flare.

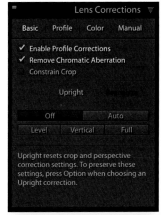

FIGURE 2.2 The Basic, Profile, and Color tabs in the Lens Corrections panel.

FIGURE 2.3 If the capture image contains an embedded profile tag, you'll see the above message in the Profile tab section of the Lens Corrections panel.

Lens profiles

By applying lens correction adjustments in Lightroom or Camera Raw, you can effectively improve the performance of any lens, providing you are able to edit the original full-frame digital capture (ideally working from a raw original). You can do this via the Manual tab of the Lens Corrections panel, but a better solution is to simply check Enable Profile Corrections and Remove Chromatic Aberration in the Basic tab section, also duplicated in the Profile tab section (see **Figure 2.2**). If the lens you shot with is one that is supported by the Lightroom/Camera Raw lens profile database, this instantly applies a geometric and lens vignetting correction. The same check box option is available in the Profile tab section, which, when enabled, shows the lens profile details confirming the make and model of lens and which specific profile has been used (you do have the option of selecting custom profiles where these are available). These corrections can make a noticeable improvement. With some camera images, you may see the message shown in **Figure 2.3**. Where the camera file already contains an embedded profile there is no need to apply one, hence there is no need to check the Enable Profile Corrections box. Some camera manufacturers, such as Panasonic and Sony (for example, the Panasonic DMC-LX3 and Sony RX100), store lens-corrected linear raw data that is already optically corrected for geometric distortion and vignetting. In these instances, Lightroom and Camera Raw know to disable the lens profile correction options because they are not needed.

Lens corrections are also available via the Lens Correction filter in Photoshop. This makes use of the same lens profile database. To use it effectively, you must remember not to crop the image before you apply the filter. You can also apply lens corrections as a smart filter in Photoshop (either via the Lens Correction filter or via the Camera Raw filter). This means you can even apply lens profile corrections to movie clips that are edited in Photoshop.

The Remove Chromatic Aberration option works independently of the lens profile and can be applied to any image, whether it is a full-frame original or has been cropped. There are no slider options to control the fringing. Checking this box is all you need to do to correct for lateral chromatic aberration. However, with axial chromatic aberration, the Defringe controls on the Color tab allow you to dial in the desired amount of defringing required to remove the purple and green hue fringing as well as edit the hue slider ranges. For more details on how to do this, see the following section, "Fixing Axial Chromatic Aberrations."

Fixing Axial Chromatic Aberrations

1 Here is a before version of the image I was about to process. I specifically wanted to emphasize the typical problems associated with axial chromatic aberration. I therefore photographed these coins using a macro-enabled lens at the widest aperture setting. I also deliberately increased the Vibrance setting in the Basic panel in order to make the fringing problem more noticeable.

2 The first step was to go to the Lens Corrections panel and check the Enable Profile Corrections box in the Profile tab. This applied a profiled lens correction based on the known lens data information. The camera body also has to be taken into account when calculating the lens profile correction to apply. For example, lenses designed for full-frame sensors can be used with both full-frame sensor cameras as well as compact dSLR cameras where the sensor size is smaller.

3 I then went to the Color tab in the Lens Corrections panel and checked the Remove Chromatic Aberration box. This auto-calculates the required color fringing correction needed. In this instance, it didn't make much difference to the color fringing.

4 This is where the Defringe sliders are needed because the fringing seen here is the result of axial rather than lateral chromatic aberrations. I began by correcting the purple fringing. I held down the Alt key and dragged on the two Purple Hue color ramp sliders. When the Alt key was held down, the affected colors appeared overlaid with black in the preview. This allowed me to fine-tune the two sliders to determine the precise color range for the purple fringing.

5 I again held down the [Alt] key as I adjusted the Purple Amount slider. In this case, the preview revealed the pixels that would be affected by the adjustment and all others were displayed as white. I could therefore determine the correct amount to apply as I increased the slider Amount setting.

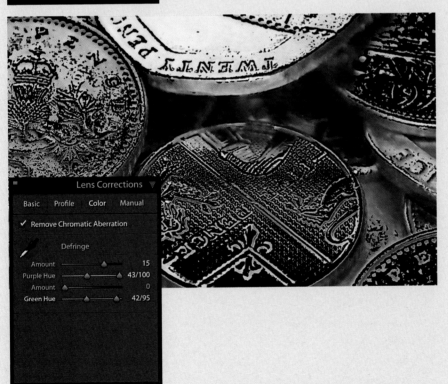

6 I then did the same thing with the Green Hue sliders. I again held down the [Alt] key as I dragged each slider. In this instance, the affected green hue colors appeared overlaid with black.

7 Likewise, I held down the Alt key as I dragged the green Amount slider, and the preview showed all the pixels that would be affected by a Green defringe adjustment and all others were displayed as white.

8 By this stage, the Lens Corrections adjustments had successfully removed all the chromatic aberrations from the photograph, including the tricky axial chromatic aberration fringing. I now went to the Detail panel and applied an appropriate amount of capture sharpening to accentuate the fine detail in the coins.

When to apply the lens corrections

When you bring a raw photo into Lightroom, it does not necessarily matter which order you apply the image adjustments in, although it usually helps to apply the lens corrections early on before you adjust anything else. If you want to apply an upright lens correction adjustment, it is best to do this first as well, but I'll explain about that more in Chapter 5. You can even configure Lightroom to do this automatically as the camera files are imported. This can be done by enabling the lens profile corrections as part of the camera default settings. If you open the Lightroom Presets preferences (see **Figure 2.4**), there is an option to "Make defaults specific to camera serial

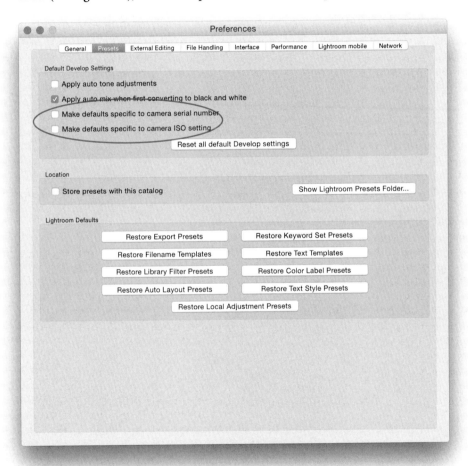

FIGURE 2.4 The Presets preferences, which can be used to establish how default camera settings are matched—either to all cameras of the same type, or to a specific camera serial number—and also whether to match all ISO settings or specific ISO settings.

number" and "Make defaults specific to camera ISO setting." After that, apply just the minimum settings to a camera image (such as lens corrections settings), and in the Develop module, choose Develop ⇨ Set Default Settings. This opens the dialog shown in **Figure 2.5**, where there is the option to click Update to Current Settings. This ensures that the settings you have configured for the selected file are recorded as the new default and applied to all newly imported files according to the rules configured in the Lightroom Presets preferences.

For example, the preferences options highlighted here allow you to customize the Set Default Develop Settings command. Setting the default settings to specific camera serial numbers allows you to save defaults for different camera bodies. You may want to carry out a custom calibration for each and therefore have the ability to assign different camera profiles. Linking the defaults to different ISO settings can be useful if you want to establish custom default Detail panel settings with the noise reduction settings best suited for specific high ISO capture settings. Just be aware that these changes are undoable, so if you already have default settings established for a particular camera, or camera plus ISO setting, setting a new default setting cannot be undone. If necessary, you can click on the Restore Adobe Default Settings button to restore the defaults completely.

FIGURE 2.5 The Set Default Develop Settings dialog.

ISO SETTING

If you need to shoot at a faster shutter speed but are unable to open up the aperture any further, a better solution is to increase the ISO speed. Now, it used to be the case that increasing the ISO speed risked degrading the image quality, so there was always a trade-off between shooting at a low ISO to capture potentially sharper images and the likelihood that camera shake or subject movement would result in a soft-looking image. Now, it is possible to have the best of all worlds. On many of the latest cameras you can safely increase the ISO speed setting, set the shutter speed setting to whatever you want, and guarantee getting a sharp, usable image. This is particularly important for sports and wildlife photographers working with long focus lenses who have a restricted lens aperture range and need to shoot using fast shutter speeds.

If you shoot raw, the only thing you will need to concern yourself with is the ISO setting. This is like an amplifier control that governs the sensitivity of the analog sensor, because interestingly, camera sensors are not actually digital but are instead analog devices. It is the analog to digital (A/D) converter that's built into the camera that converts the analog signal into a digital output. The sensor will have an optimum ISO setting at which it performs best, and the ISO control can be used to turn the sensitivity up or down depending on which setting you choose. This is something that can't be manipulated later and is fixed at the time of capture whether you shoot raw or JPEG.

When shooting film, the slower ISO emulsions always recorded the finest grain detail and were considered best for detailed photography. In the case of digital, turning down the ISO sensitivity doesn't always equate to finer-quality images. If you want the best tone image quality, you should set the camera to its optimum, native ISO setting, which may be something like 100, 160, or 200. This is the setting at which the analog sensor performs best, as a correctly exposed image shot at this setting will produce an optimum dynamic range image with the least amount of noise. If you set the camera to a lower than native ISO setting, this can be just as bad as selecting a higher ISO, because the photosites on the sensor will become overwhelmed with light and the gain applied to the sensor has to be turned down below the optimal level to compensate. This can result in images that are slightly more grainy. If you choose to increase the ISO setting and do so by selecting an in-between setting such as 500 ISO, this is effectively a digitally enhanced setting, which may produce more noise in the image than if you had increased the setting to 800 ISO instead. As a consequence, the general advice is that when you increase the ISO setting, you should do so by doubling the native ISO. On Canon cameras, the native ISO will most likely be 100, so the best settings to use are 200, then 400, followed by 800. On Nikon cameras, you'll usually find the native ISO is 160, and therefore optimal settings are 320, then 640, and so on.

NOTE

The camera's onboard processer is used to read the digital image data, generate the thumbnail view seen on the LCD display, and process the image to generate rendered JPEG versions. The camera menu controls therefore determine things like what white balance, color profile, noise reduction, and sharpening are applied when generating a JPEG output.

CAPTURE SHARPENING

All images require some degree of sharpening to be applied at the capture stage, as without such sharpening they would look rather soft. For example, if you shoot using a JPEG mode setting, your camera's onboard image processor applies the sharpening automatically. If you shoot using the raw mode, no sharpening is applied and it will be left to you to determine the required amount of sharpening that's needed. In the case of Camera Raw and Lightroom, the Detail panel settings have evolved over the last few versions to offer a comprehensive set of sliders that allow you to control both the sharpening and noise reduction (**Figure 2.6**). With all this choice comes the need to understand how these controls should be used to their best effect.

Capture sharpening is basically about applying just the right amount of sharpening to compensate for the inherent lack of sharpness in a raw master image. With all raw processing programs, including Lightroom and Camera Raw, a default amount of sharpening is applied to raw images. Some raw processing programs may show a zero setting for the sharpness slider, whereas in fact a certain amount of sharpening may already have been applied under the hood. To see what I mean, open a raw image, set the zoom view to 100% (or 200% on a HiDPI display), go to the Detail panel in the Develop module, and set the Sharpening slider to zero. If you toggle between the default sharpening and the zero setting, you should see quite a difference in the image's appearance.

How you configure the remaining sliders here—Radius, Detail, and Masking—will be based on a subjective analysis of the image. The default settings shown in Figure 2.6 are a good starting point for any image, but you can refine these according to the actual image content. For example, fine detailed images look best when using a low radius of, say, 0.7, and soft detail images, such as portraits, are best sharpened using a higher radius of, say, 1.3. With images that have been shot at a low ISO setting, you can push the Detail slider all the way up to 100, but with higher ISO settings it is best to keep the Detail amount closer to the default setting of 25. The Masking slider can be used to filter the sharpening effect so that when you apply a high Masking amount, the sharpening is concentrated to the edges only. At a zero setting, no masking is applied at all. With detailed landscapes, it is best to use a zero or low Masking setting. With portrait photographs, it is better to use a higher Masking setting to preserve the skin tones from being oversharpened.

Capture Sharpening workflow

1 This shows a close-up view of a photograph I took of a flamingo. Below is a 200% view where the Detail panel Sharpening Amount slider was set to zero. This shows what the original raw image looked like without any presharpening applied. It's obviously a little soft, but this is only to be expected. All raw images require a certain amount of presharpening. The trick is knowing what are the optimum settings for an individual image.

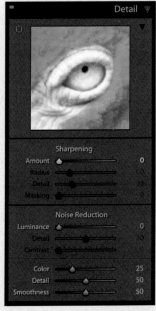

2 In this step I set the Amount slider to 50, which is a little higher than you would apply normally. I set the Radius slider to the minimum 0.5 setting and captured the screen shot shown below by holding down the [Alt] key to display a grayscale preview of the sharpening effect. This allowed me to preview the effect of the Radius slider setting in isolation. It is best to set the preview to 100% or higher when analyzing a grayscale preview of the sharpening effect.

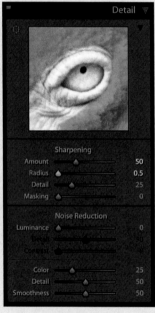

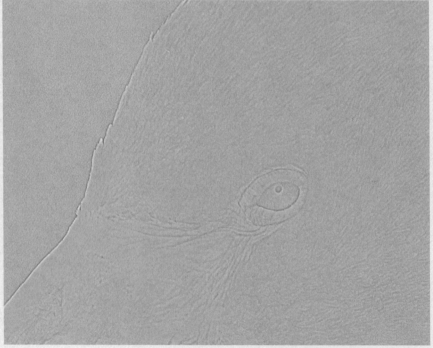

3 I then dragged the Radius slider to the maximum 3.0 setting and again held down the [Alt] key to see a grayscale preview using this Radius setting. While the narrow Radius setting didn't do that much, the high Radius setting emphasized just the wide edge features, such as the eye and the outline edge of the bird. The ideal setting will always be somewhere between these two extremes.

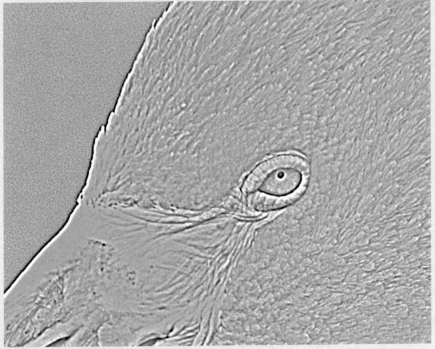

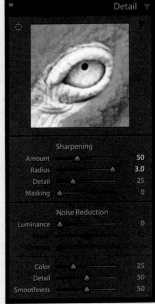

4 For this image, I felt the optimum Radius setting would be 0.9, as this was the right amount to emphasize the edges of the feathers. Next, I wanted to adjust the Detail slider. Increasing the Detail slider amount from the default 25 setting strengthens the halo edges and results in a more pronounced sharpening effect. Shown below is a grayscale preview of the Detail effect captured with the [Alt] key held down. If you inspect closely, you will notice that while the detail on the flamingo now looks nice and crisp, the sharpening settings have also ended up emphasizing the luminance pattern noise, and this is most clearly visible in the green background.

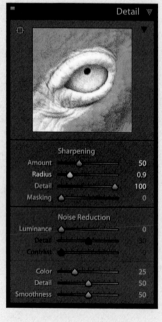

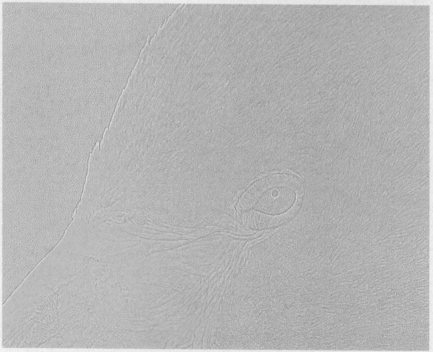

5 To address this problem, I adjusted the Masking slider, and as I did so held down the [Alt] key in order to see a grayscale preview, which showed what the mask looked like. As you increase the Masking setting, this increases the size of the black mask areas, indicating which portions of the image are being protected from being sharpened. In this instance, I reckoned a Mask amount of 50 did a good job of protecting the green background areas from being oversharpened, while the white areas in the mask preview represented the areas where the sharpening would be applied most.

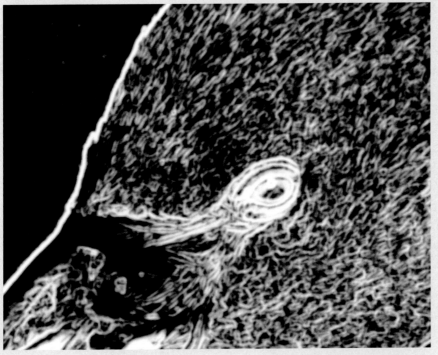

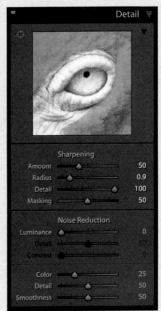

6 Finally, I went back to the Basic panel and adjusted the Clarity slider. Adding more Clarity allowed me to increase the midtone contrast, which helped reveal more texture detail in the midtone areas. In this instance, I set the Clarity slider to +20, which was just enough to bring out more detail in the feathers.

NOISE REDUCTION

As you raise the gain applied to the sensor signal (by increasing the ISO), you heighten its sensitivity, which therefore amplifies the underlying noise. Increasing the ISO setting also causes the dynamic range of the sensor to decrease. So ideally, you don't want to push the ISO too high unless you have to, even though modern sensors can now produce much smoother images at the higher ISO settings. As you push the ISO to the point where noise becomes noticeable, this can be addressed by applying noise reduction via the Detail panel (**Figure 2.7**).

Now, the thing to bear in mind here is that when you apply any kind of noise reduction, the image is going to be softened to some extent. So, there has to be a balance struck between applying enough noise reduction to smooth out any noise that is obtrusive and sharpening the image using the Sharpening controls, which in turn will emphasize any noise that's still present. The best advice I can give is to start by adjusting the Luminance slider. This can be used to suppress the luminance, or pattern noise that has a film grain type of appearance. Raise the amount just enough to get rid of most of the noise without trying to obtain a perfectly smooth look—the less you have to increase the Luminance slider, the better. You can follow this with adjustments to the Detail slider. This acts as a threshold control for the Luminance noise reduction slide, where the default setting is set midway at 50. Dragging to the right will reduce the amount of smoothing and preserve more detail. Dragging to the left will cause more detailed areas to be inappropriately detected as noise and result in a smoother-looking image. Increasing the amount setting for the Contrast slider can help restore more contrast at the macro level. It is more effective when the Luminance Detail slider is set to a low value (thereby raising the threshold for the areas that should be regarded as noise). Adding more contrast can help disguise the smoothing effects of the Luminance and Detail sliders, but the effect is rather subtle compared with the power of the other two main sliders.

As the levels of light drop, the sensor will be less able to differentiate color because the luminance is so low. This results in errors in the way color is recorded, which can be seen as colored speckles in the demosaiced image. By default, Lightroom and Camera Raw apply a Color noise reduction setting of 25. This is minimal enough to have no adverse effect on photographs shot at a low ISO but is sufficient to remove most of the noticeable color noise that can occur when shooting at higher ISO settings. If you select a high ISO image and disable the noise reduction, you will certainly see a difference between the standard corrected and uncorrected versions. Applying higher amounts of Color noise reduction may be necessary with very high ISO shots but can result in the colors bleeding around the sharp edges. You can compensate for this by adjusting the Detail slider (below the Color slider). Dragging the slider to the right prevents bleed at the expense of emphasizing the underlying pattern noise. The Smoothness slider is designed to handle low-frequency color noise, which can be present in low as well as high ISO images.

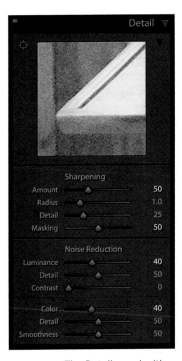

FIGURE 2.7 The Detail panel with the Noise Reduction settings adjusted to help improve the appearance of an image shot at a high ISO setting.

HOW TO REMOVE MOIRÉ PATTERNS

The following steps show how it is possible to remove moiré effects from an image when editing in Lightroom. Moiré is the term used to describe image artifacts that are caused as a result of light interference. This can be due to the way light reflected from a fine pattern subject causes interference patterns to appear in the final capture. If the frequency of the subject pattern and the frequency of the photosites on the sensor clash, this can result in an amplified moiré pattern. Most camera sensors feature a high-pass, anti-aliasing filter that covers the sensor and introduces a very slight amount of image detail softening to mitigate some of the effects of moiré. Most of the time, high-pass filters do a good job of preventing moiré, though occasionally, such as in the example shown here, it won't always prevent moiré effects from being seen in the final image. For example, when Nikon launched the D800 camera, it came with a D800E variant where the anti-aliasing filter covering the sensor was removed and its successor, the Nikon D810, also omits an anti-aliasing filter, as do the Sony A7r models. Removing the anti-aliasing filter results in sharper captures, or at least captures that require less software capture sharpening, at the expense of becoming more prone to moiré problems. As you can see in the following steps, where moiré does become noticeable it is now possible to fix it in Lightroom using a localized adjustment method. The only downside is that the moiré reduction processing is very processor-intensive and can cause subsequent raw processing to slow down. This is why it's best to carry out this step last.

1 This shows the uncropped version of the photograph I took of the Chicago skyline from Northerly Island. I wanted the focus to be on the shoreline and buildings, so I selected the crop overlay tool in the Develop module and clicked and dragged to define the area I wanted to crop to.

2 In this close-up view, you can clearly see a moiré pattern on the building in the middle.

3 I selected the adjustment brush and set the Moiré slider to +100 (this is the setting you need to use when you want to remove moiré). I then brushed over the building to get rid of all traces of the moiré artifacts.

"Exposing to the right" is an approach that's recommended if you wish to achieve the optimum exposure when shooting digitally. This is done by setting the exposure to the brightest setting possible before the highlights start to clip. This exposure setting might agree with what the camera meter is telling you, or it might be a stop or more brighter. The most effective way to check is to shoot in tethered mode and use the Lightroom Develop module Histogram panel to gauge if this is the case. This method allows you to set the exposure precisely to record the optimum number of levels data but is only really applicable for studio shooting. When shooting untethered on location, you can't rely on the camera histogram, so the only option is to use your intuition regarding the amount it is OK to overexpose or to bracket the exposures as you shoot. Afterward, you can select the lightest, most usable exposure to edit.

TONE CAPTURE

A digital camera records light values in a linear fashion. Once a sensor image has been converted digitally, you will notice that for each stop increase in exposure, you double the amount of light hitting the sensor and it records twice as many levels, up to the point where, as the exposure brightness is increased, the sensor starts to clip the brightest portions of the image. Put simply, with a normal exposed image the most detailed information (the most levels of data) will be recorded at the highlight end. If a highlight area appears overexposed, you stand a good chance of recovering lots of detail in the highlights so long as no important highlight tone areas are clipped in two or more channels. Meanwhile, the least detailed information (the fewest levels of data) will be recorded at the shadow end. In extreme cases you will notice that there are real limits as to how much detail you can rescue in the shadows without seeing severe banding or noise.

Between these two extremes is the range of usable tones that a camera can capture, which is referred to as the dynamic range of the sensor. This can be determined by measuring the point at which usable data can be read at the shadow end to the point where usable data can be read at the highlight end. For example, DXO Labs applies a standardized approach that is probably similar to this for all the camera sensors it tests and is thereby able to quantify the dynamic range of each sensor. At the time of writing this book, the sensors tested that have the best dynamic range are the Nikon D810 and Red Epic Dragon, with dynamic range ratings of 14.8 EVs (this stands for Exposure Values, or stops of exposure). This is a major improvement upon early dSLR cameras that typically had dynamic ranges of around 10 to 11 EVs. When using a camera that has increased dynamic range, there is more latitude when selecting the exposure as well as extending the range of tones that can be usefully be edited at the postprocessing stage. Photographers can also extend the dynamic range of their camera by shooting bracketed exposures, shooting two or more photos at 2 EVs apart, and then blending them using a variety of postprocessing techniques (some of which are described later in this book). However, it is still important to get the exposure right at the time you capture the photograph. If you bear in mind that the most detailed tonal information is captured at the highlight end, then the most logical approach is to follow the "expose to the right" rule.

It is OK to clip the shadows or highlights

Just because modern digital sensors give you the scope to simultaneously expand the tones in the highlights and the shadows doesn't mean you should. When the balancing of the shadows and highlights is taken to extremes, the results can look rather odd, hence the backlash against over-the-top High Dynamic Range (HDR) image processing. It is worth remembering that it is OK to sometimes let the shadows or highlights appear compressed or even clipped. In fact, some photographs will look

1 Here is a photograph shot on a bright sunny day, shown with the default tone settings applied. The problem is that the highlights appear somewhat blown out and the shadow detail is hidden.

2 When we view such a scene, our eyes naturally adjust and compensate for the differing levels of brightness. For example, when we look at the trees, we perceive them to look like the cropped section shown on the left. Likewise, when we look at the brighter areas such as the church tower, our eyes compensate so that we perceive this to look like the cropped section shown on the right.

3 When editing a capture like this, the main thing is to choose an exposure that records the tones that are most important. In this case, it would be best to expose to record as bright an exposure as possible, but without any of the highlights clipping. While it may be possible to balance the shadows and highlights as shown in Step 2, the ideal adjustment will be to contain all the important highlight detail and preserve all the important shadow detail as well, but not overlighten to the point where the shadows look artificial.

better if you concentrate on enhancing just a narrow range of tones within the original scene. While image-capture methods may have changed over the last few decades, printed images have more or less the same dynamic range as those that were produced in a darkroom. Basically, the question of how to get from point A (the subject scene) to point B (the printed representation) is not much different now from how it's always been. The problem is that with so many new tools to control the tone and color and every stage, we sometimes find ourselves getting lost in endless possibilities. The desire to enhance everything is strong, but if you try to show everything, you can end up with an image that just looks dull and flat or has hideous halo artifacts.

HDR techniques still have their place and are used more widely than you think—there are photographers using these techniques to produce images that you wouldn't have guessed had been processed in this way. HDR image-processing techniques have become a lot more refined in recent years. If you are shooting a landscape subject and you think increasing the dynamic range will be useful, it is always a good idea to shoot a bracketed set of exposures using either three or five images shot two stops apart. Often I find the normal exposure image contains all the tonal information I need, but it's nice to have the source images available to expand the dynamic range further should the need arise. My own early experiments with HDR were not that successful, but I am still glad that I took the time to take those extra shots because the HDR blending techniques that are available now work much better at rendering natural-looking photographs.

Bit depth

The bit depth is the number of bits or discrete levels of tone information in a digital image. For example, the sensors in older digital cameras may have a bit depth of 12 bits, which is 2 to the power of 12, or 4,000 levels per channel, while the sensors in more recent dSLRs are capable of capturing 14 bits of data, or 16,000 levels per channel. Where you have a sensor that is capable of capturing a high dynamic range, a higher bit depth provides more tonal levels, and the ability to capture more bits should translate to smoother tonal gradation and less risk of posterization. Something to bear in mind, though, is the background noise signature of the sensor. A higher bit depth won't improve the image quality if the presence of noise masks whatever benefits the higher bit-depth capture can offer. For practical purposes, 12 bits is all most sensors are actually capable of, though there are exceptions; some of the latest sensors are starting to break through this barrier, and there is a true benefit in being able to capture 14 bits of data. This is because the underlying noise signature is very low, and there is an appreciable difference when shooting at the native ISO setting.

Bit depth can also refer to the bit depth of composite color channels. For instance, an 8-bit-per-channel image can also be described as a 24-bit composite RGB image. Likewise, a 16-bit-per-channel image can be described as a 48-bit composite RGB image. So, it can be confusing if it is not made clear whether the bit depth refers to the single channel bit depth or the composite color channels. It is more common to refer to the channel bit depth.

Typically, the raw data captured by a digital sensor will contain at least 12 bits of editable data, or up to 4,000 usable levels of information. Lightroom carries out all the editing in 16 bit (some of the internal processing steps are even in 32 bit). So when you capture a raw image and process it in Lightroom, all the bits are preserved as much as possible. Since the processing is carried out in a bit depth greater than any current digital camera can capture, this ensures all the levels of data are preserved as much as possible as you carry out your Lightroom edits. If you capture an image in JPEG mode, then you will be already limited to the bit depth of the JPEG format, which is 8 bit, which means a camera JPEG capture will always be limited to 256 levels per channel. This is why it is always advisable to shoot in raw mode, because you have not just the freedom to fully edit the Develop settings, but you will preserve much more of the tonal information.

When you export an image from Lightroom, either as a rendered output image or to carry on editing in Photoshop, you have the option to choose whether to export as an 8-bit or 16-bit image. JPEGs can only be saved as 8 bit, whereas you can use the PSD or TIFF formats to save as 8 bit or 16 bit. In each case, the number of levels contained in the exported file are likely to be less than in the original. This is because color and tonal editing involves manipulating the original levels in the master such that some areas of the rendered output image will end up more compressed and others more stretched. So the exported output file is bound to have fewer levels than the original it came from. In the case of camera JPEG originals that have been edited in Lightroom and exported as 8-bit files, there will always be less than 256 levels per channel in the output version. It can be argued that if you optimize a raw file in Lightroom and export as an 8-bit JPEG or TIFF, while being limited to 256 levels per channel, this will be a fully optimized image in no further need of correction, and therefore 8 bits per channel is more than enough to display such an image on a web page or place it in a print layout. However, if you intend to carry out any further image-editing work in Photoshop, it's best to always export in 16 bit, because you can continue to preserve all the original levels data when working in Photoshop. When exporting raw originals as a 16-bit TIFF or PSD, the output version will contain the maximum number of levels possible. So while it may not have as many as 4,000 levels, it will still be significantly more than if you had exported as an 8-bit image.

NOTE

When exporting from Lightroom or editing in Photoshop, the bit depth choice will either be 8 bit or 16 bit. JPEG photos are captured in 8 bit, so there is no point in switching from 8 bit to 16 bit (because if you pour a half pint into a pint jug, you still end up with just a half pint of liquid). If the source image contains more than 8 bits of data, such as a 12-bit raw file, you will gain by saving that image as a 16-bit TIFF in order to contain the extra bits.

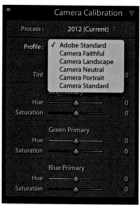

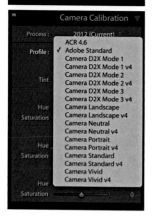

FIGURE 2.8 The Camera Calibration panel showing the Profile options for a Canon EOS camera (top), Fujifilm X-Pro1 (middle), and Nikon D700 (bottom).

The downside of exporting and editing in 16 bit is that the file size of a 16-bit file will be twice that of an 8-bit image, although the additional cost of disk space is less of an issue given today's generous storage systems. Also, when managing your files in Lightroom, it is only with the hero master shots—in particular, those that require additional editing in Photoshop—that it will be necessary to generate a 16-bit derivative file from the raw file format. Sixteen-bit images also take longer to save and open, which again is less of a problem than it once was. Larger files will take longer to upload to and download from a server, but at the final output stage it is more likely you will want to export as 8 bit. For example, all the essential image-editing work I do is carried out in Lightroom, followed, when necessary, in Photoshop as 16-bit TIFFs. When I prepare files for use in a book such as this, I export them as 8-bit TIFFs because 16 bit would be overkill when no further image editing is required, and I need the upload/download times to be as manageable as possible.

LIGHTROOM RAW PROCESSING

When you shoot in raw mode, the only consideration is the framing, making sure the image is sharp where it needs to be and selecting the most appropriate ISO, shutter speed, and lens aperture. If you choose to shoot in JPEG mode, a lot of controls can be configured on the camera itself, from the type of "color look" to the amount of noise reduction and sharpening that's applied. When shooting raw, all these controls are redundant apart from the ability to select an appropriate white balance setting, which can easily be overridden at the raw processing stage.

CALIBRATION SETTINGS

One of the first things you'll notice as you import the photos into Lightroom is how the image thumbnails start out as one color and then all of a sudden refresh to produce different-looking color thumbnails (and previews). This is because when you shoot in raw mode, the camera also generates a JPEG preview and embeds it in the header section of the raw file. This JPEG preview is what you see when you preview an image on the LCD screen of the camera. It is also used to calculate the LCD histogram display, which is why the histogram you see on the back of the camera is really only an approximate representation of what the camera has captured as raw data. Overexposure warnings should therefore be taken with a pinch of salt. It may be in some cases the file is so overexposed in some areas you won't be able to see any detail, but more often than not you will be able to render perfect tone information in the flagged areas.

The preview the camera embeds is the one Lightroom uses to generate the initial Library module previews. Chances are, if you go to the Camera Calibration panel, you'll see you have Adobe Standard selected as the current camera sensor profile (see **Figure 2.8**). The options you see in this section depend on the type of camera used. There will always be an Adobe Standard option, and this is a camera profile that is provided as a calibration standard, established by the Camera Raw team at Adobe. In some instances this profile is based on an aggregate of camera samples tested, and the intention is to provide a suitable baseline for Lightroom and Camera Raw image adjustments starting from a calibrated, color-neutral starting point. You may also see listed a Camera Standard profile. This is designed to match the default preview rendering you see when you first import the raw files, where the default camera standard look has been selected. The other camera profile options will vary depending on the camera used. These profiles are designed to match the other camera menu option looks available for each camera. So, if you find the jump in appearance disconcerting when you import your raw photos and you happen to prefer the embedded JPEG preview look, you can match this by selecting the Camera Standard option from the Profile menu and, as mentioned earlier, include this as part of the default Develop setting. Or, let's say you like the Camera Landscape or Camera Velvia/Vivid look as your starting point; select this and, if desired, set it as the default Develop setting for this camera.

The thing to bear in mind here is that the camera profile or look you select is simply a starting point upon which to base your additional tone and color corrections. For most types of work, I recommend you select a standard profile: either the Adobe standard (which will use Adobe's own calibration for your particular camera body), or the manufacturer's Camera Standard, which will also be calibrated to your camera but most likely produce a more saturated rendering. It can produce nice-looking results, but not all subjects suit a color-enhanced interpretation. Or, you can even create a measured custom profile for your camera. For more information, check out the free DNG Profile Editor program, available from Adobe.

BASIC PANEL ADJUSTMENTS

The first main step is to optimize the tones and colors in the image. In most cases, I find it is best to adjust the Basic panel settings first to achieve a baseline setting where the tonal range is either expanded or compressed, as necessary, and the Histogram panel should show a histogram with a full distribution of tone levels. A perfect histogram does not always indicate a perfect tone balance, but it does serve as a useful starting reference point. A few Basic panel tone tweaks may be all an image needs to look great. You can even just click on the Auto tone button in the Basic panel to see what settings this gives you and whether it improves the look of the image and then fine-tune to taste. You may then wish to save a snapshot or a virtual copy.

TIP

The Develop module Presets
panel is located on the left of the
Develop module interface just
below the Navigator panel.

APPLYING CAMERA PROFILES

The Camera Calibration panel in the Develop module contains the pop-up menu shown below, where you can select the desired camera profile. You may want to establish a particular profile as part of the default Develop settings (see Figure 2.5). You can also create Develop presets in which just the camera profile setting is selected. You can then review the different camera profile options more quickly by rolling the mouse over the saved camera profile Develop presets.

1 This shows an image opened in the Lightroom Develop module where all the panels were set to their default settings. In the Camera Calibration panel, you can see the Profile options available for this Canon raw image. Adobe Standard is currently selected.

Adobe Standard   Camera Faithful   Camera Landscape

Camera Neutral   Camera Portrait   Camera Standard

2 Here you can see a comparison of the profile options available for this Canon camera. As I mentioned in Step 1, no other panel adjustments had been applied yet. The profile selection simply provides a starting point upon which to make further Develop adjustments.

Images added to the Lightroom catalog can be grouped into stacks. This can be done in the Library module by choosing Photo ⇨ Stacking ⇨ Group into Stack and undone by choosing Photo ⇨ Stacking ⇨ Unstack. It is particularly useful when you need to group together a number of associated images such as a panorama or HDR stack, as well as for time-lapse sequences where the number of images may run into the hundreds. In this section of the text, I refer to how Lightroom can be configured so that images that have been edited in an external editor are automatically stacked with the original master image.

SECONDARY DEVELOP MODULE ADJUSTMENTS

Having established the initial tone settings, you can use the Tone Curve and HSL/Color/B&W panels to further edit the image. This second stage can be like fine-tuning the initial settings to produce a more creative interpretation rather than what might be regarded as the "perfect" image-adjustment setting.

EXPORTING FROM LIGHTROOM TO PHOTOSHOP

For all the reasons I mentioned earlier, it is best to configure the External Editing preferences in Lightroom (see **Figure 2.9**) to generate 16-bit TIFF files whenever you choose Photo ⇨ Edit in ⇨ Photoshop. If an image you have captured has lots of levels of data per channel, why throw them away when you switch to editing the photo in Photoshop? If the subsequent editing you do in Photoshop involves further tone and color manipulation, even if it's only slight or is applied to localized areas, it doesn't make sense to limit the editing to 8 bit when choosing 16 bit guarantees you will preserve as much image integrity as possible.

When you choose Photo ⇨ Edit in ⇨ Photoshop, this opens a rendered version of the original image in Photoshop but does not actually save it as a new version until you choose File ⇨ Save in Photoshop. Only then do the file format and compression settings (configured in the External Editing preferences) come into play. Saving also automatically adds that version to the Lightroom catalog and saves it to the same Lightroom folder location as the original. If Stack With Original is checked (circled in Figure 2.9), the saved, rendered version will be stacked with the original. However, this assumes the versions of Lightroom and Photoshop you are using are both compatible or up-to-date. If you are using Lightroom CC with Photoshop CC, the obvious solution is to check that you have installed the latest updates for both programs. But if you are using, say, a perpetual license version of Photoshop for which there is no current update to match the version of Lightroom you are using, you will be faced with a dialog such as the one shown in **Figure 2.10**, where you have several choices. Open Anyway instructs Photoshop to open the image directly without saving. This will work fine as long as you have not applied any edit adjustments in Lightroom that will be incompatible with the Camera Raw plug-in used in your version of Photoshop. If this is going to be an issue, you can choose Render in Lightroom. This uses the Camera Raw engine in Lightroom to create a rendered copy that can then be opened in Photoshop. So the difference here is that in such circumstances choosing Photo ⇨ Edit in ⇨ Photoshop (followed by clicking Render in Lightroom) will always create a rendered file copy in the process.

There is also an option to open files from Lightroom in an external editing program. You'll see this option in the External Editing preferences, and the settings you select here are reflected in the Lightroom Photo ⇨ Edit in menu, where the program

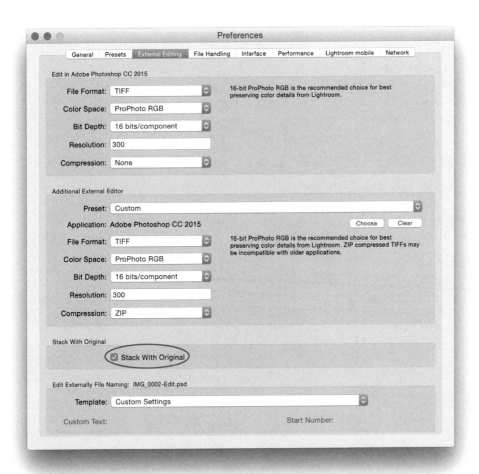

FIGURE 2.9 The Lightroom External Editing preferences, where you can establish the settings to be used when creating a rendered image for editing in Photoshop or another external program.

FIGURE 2.10 The dialog you will see if there is a mismatch between the versions of Camera Raw used by Lightroom and Photoshop.

FIGURE 2.11 You can open a raw photo from Lightroom as a smart object in Photoshop. In this Layers panel view, you can see the image layer has a smart object icon: double-clicking this opens the Camera Raw dialog to reveal and give you access to the applied Lightroom Develop module settings. In Photoshop you can apply filters to smart objects. In this example, you can see I applied a Blur Gallery filter to a raw image smart object.

settings you configure in the preferences will be shown listed. For example, you might wish to have the option to render your Lightroom files in an older version of Photoshop, or some other pixel-editing program. The preferences can also be configured to open your images in the same version of Photoshop, but using different TIFF file compression or bit-depth options. Whatever you do, choosing Photo ⇨ Edit in ⇨ [selected external editing program], or using the shortcut ⌘ Alt E (Mac), Ctrl Alt E (PC), will always produce a rendered version, saved to the same folder as the original master image.

To sum up, choosing Photo ⇨ Edit in ⇨ Photoshop (⌘ E [Mac], Ctrl E [PC]) normally opens the raw file directly in Photoshop as an unsaved rendered image ready to be edited. If you close the image without saving it, the file closes without being added to the catalog. If you choose File ⇨ Save in Photoshop, it then saves the image using the Lightroom External Editor configured settings and adds it to the Lightroom catalog in the same folder location as the original. Choosing Photo ⇨ Edit in ⇨ external editor (⌘ Alt E [Mac], Ctrl Alt E [PC]) always generates a saved rendered file in the same folder location as the original using whatever settings have been configured in the Lightroom External Editor settings.

PHOTOSHOP IMAGE EDITING

When editing raw files, the ideal approach is to carry out as much of the editing as you can in Lightroom and only export the files to Photoshop when it is necessary to retouch them further. These days you can do a lot in Lightroom without ever needing to use Photoshop. You can add localized adjustments and remove objects, but for complex image-editing jobs, it will always be faster and more effective to leave Lightroom at some point and take your file into Photoshop to do the heavy-duty retouching.

My preference is to keep the image-edit retouching as nondestructive as possible at every stage. When you choose to edit an image in Photoshop, or export a photo as a TIFF file and edit it, you can't then go back to Lightroom and readjust the original Develop settings because the edit settings become fixed when you create a rendered TIFF image. Once you export a file in this way, whatever retouching work you do in Photoshop is done from that baseline starting point.

Having said that, it is possible to export photos from Lightroom as smart objects. In this workflow you can select a raw photo in Lightroom, go to the Photo ⇨ Edit menu, and choose Open as Smart Object in Photoshop. This allows you to open a raw image from Lightroom into Photoshop and keep it in a raw image state (see **Figure 2.11**). If you do this and double-click the smart object layer, it will open the Camera Raw dialog, which will provide you with access to the same Camera Raw settings that were applied in Lightroom. This workflow allows you to open a photo in Photoshop and retain the ability to edit the Camera Raw/Develop settings. You can edit a raw smart object photo in Photoshop and apply most Photoshop image adjustments and filters and still be able to re-edit the underlying raw settings. The problem is, when you do this it can really slow things down, and the onscreen updates will take a while to refresh each time you update the underlying Camera Raw settings. More importantly, should you use any of the Photoshop retouching tools on an empty new layer (such as the spot healing brush or brush tool), you can't then update the settings for the underlying smart object layer because this will render all the brushwork on the layers above obsolete. There are some instances where it is useful to open raw images as smart object layers in Photoshop, but because of the above limitations it is not something that is always practical or particularly helpful when you switch from editing in Lightroom to editing in Photoshop. However, smart objects/smart filters are still very useful for some specific Photoshop image-editing tasks.

Adjustment layers

The easiest way to keep your Photoshop image editing nondestructive is to make full use of layers and adjustment layers. The clone stamp and healing work is best applied first on an empty new layer just above the image background layer. If you need to carry out further retouching work on any areas of an image that have already been worked on, you may want to fix the work done so far as a merged visible layer and carry on editing. For example, you can clone unwanted blemishes first, fix the retouching work by merging the visible layers to a new layer above, and then proceed to edit using the brush tool, say, and then fade the layer opacity to blend the paintbrush work with the spotting work. Adjustment layers should ideally be placed above the pixel retouching layers, where they can be applied either to the layer immediately below (in what is called a clipping group) or to all visible layers below, or masked so they are applied to selected areas only. **Figure 2.12** shows an example of a simple layer stack where the Spotting layer is immediately above the Background layer, the Painting layer is above the Spotting layer (with the layer opacity faded to 70%) and lastly, a masked Curves adjustment layer is added last at the top of the layer stack. This demonstrates some of the fundamental principles of Photoshop layers, whether the job you are doing is fairly simple or you're creating more complex image composites.

It is also a good idea to minimize the number of adjustment layers used. When multiple, global adjustment layers are added to an image and you choose to flatten all the layers, the result is a cumulative series of adjustments, rather than a merged blend. For example, if you add a Curves layer on top of a Levels on top of a Brightness and Contrast adjustment layer and flatten to merge, the result is the same as if you opened an image, applied a Brightness and Contrast adjustment, then applied a Levels adjustment and a Curves adjustment. Clearly this is not good practice, as the image is progressively degraded at each step. If you consider that Brightness

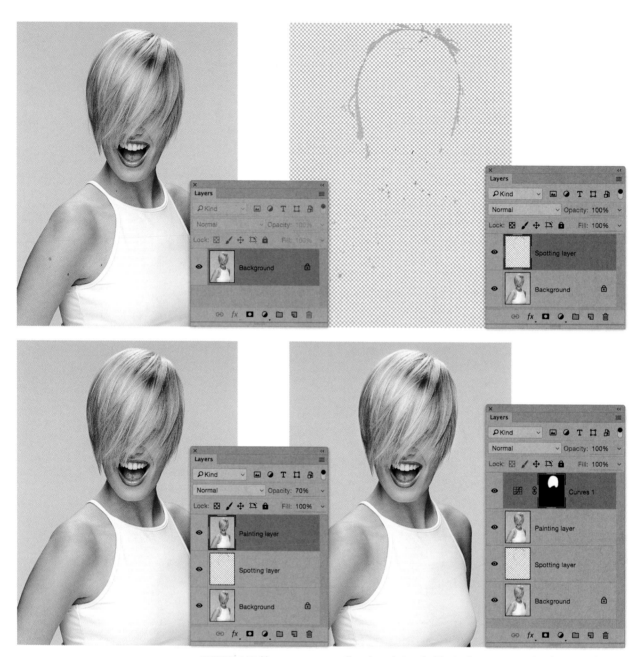

FIGURE 2.12 Here you can see the steps taken in Photoshop to retouch a beauty photo. At the top left, you see the optimized image exported from Lightroom with just a Background layer. Next to that, a spotting layer was added. At the bottom left, a merged composite layer was edited using the brush tool, where the layer opacity was set to 70%. Next to that is the final version with a masked Curves adjustment layer at the top of the layer stack.

and Contrast, Levels, and Curves adjustments can all be summarized with a single Curves adjustment, the ideal solution is to reduce everything to a single Curves adjustment. It is not quite the same if you apply masked layer adjustments, because here you are using adjustment layers to adjust distinct areas of an image, rather than applying a global adjustment. You will often see retouched images where lots of adjustment layers have been added, but because each adjustment layer relates to a small area of the image, it does not have an adverse effect on the image as a whole when the layers are all flattened.

Continued editing in Lightroom

Each time you save an image that has been edited in Photoshop, Lightroom will update the preview for the rendered pixel image that's been added to the catalog. Once the Photoshop editing has been completed, there may be nothing more that needs to be done to that image. If a photo does happen to need a little more work, there is the option to reopen the image in Photoshop and edit it further, but instead, you can always make those adjustments in Lightroom.

What you decide to do here depends on your preferred image-editing workflow. Some photographers feel that once you start editing an image in Photoshop, everything subsequent to that should be done in Photoshop. But once you have finished doing all the Photoshop editing and saved an image back to the Lightroom catalog, you do have the option to apply a new set of Lightroom Develop adjustments to the Photoshop-edited rendered TIFF image. What I typically do is to carry out all the initial image processing in Lightroom, edit a rendered TIFF copy in Photoshop, where I will do all the complex retouching, and save back to Lightroom, where I may carry out some further fine-tuning adjustments. For example, if you want to make a print, it is advisable to soft proof the image first before printing (which is discussed a little later in this chapter). Basically, the soft-proof process may require you to make some additional adjustments using the Lightroom Develop module controls to optimize the image before making a print. To create a black-and-white photograph, it makes sense to have a master up-to-date version that is kept in color, where the black-and-white conversion process happens last. So in these situations I will carry out the initial optimization in Lightroom, edit in Photoshop (keeping the photo in color), and save to add it to the Lightroom catalog. Once I am back in Lightroom, I can use the Black and White Mix controls in the HSL/Color/B&W panel to apply the black-and-white conversion. This way, if I decide I would prefer to use the image in color, it is a simple matter of removing the black-and-white conversion step in Lightroom, or more likely, I will create a separate snapshot or a new virtual copy so I can easily access both the color and black-and-white versions of the same image.

COLOR MANAGEMENT

In order to handle the color from one device to another, a color management system is required. In the case of Lightroom the color management is built in, so as long as your camera is supported, Lightroom knows how to interpret the raw files and show the colors correctly on the display. The sensor in your camera will most likely be able to capture more colors than can be seen on the display, in print, or with the human eye. Lightroom therefore uses a very wide gamut of RGB (Red, Green, Blue) space to manage all the internal color calculations. For those in the know, it is based on the ProPhoto RGB space, which means it can handle just about any color a camera can capture and preserve the color relationships between one color and the next without any clipping. While such a space is fine for the internal image processing, it has to be converted to a secondary RGB space to produce the image you see on the screen. The computer display you view your images with will have a more limited color gamut compared with the gamut of your camera, so the key here is to ensure the image processing does not constrain the gamut of the original (which it does by using a wide gamut RGB space) and that the image you see on the more limited gamut computer display is as accurate as possible. To achieve this, there often has to be a fair amount of color tonal compression and, sometimes, clipping to get the out-of-gamut colors to fit the smaller gamut of the display.

A basic LCD display will probably have a color gamut that is close to sRGB (standard Red Green Blue). This is considered a fairly small gamut space in which a number of colors, in particular greens and cyans, are clipped. If you edit a raw image in Lightroom using an sRGB display, the Lightroom image processing will preserve as much as possible all the colors in the master image, but you will be previewing those edits through a more limited sRGB gamut. A professional LCD monitor will have a color gamut that is close to the Adobe RGB space. This means you will be able to distinguish more color detail on the display and see a preview that matches nearly the entire gamut of a typical CMYK space. Such displays are ideal for prepress work, but also for any type of photo editing where you want optimum color display performance.

When it comes to making a print, the gamut of the printer will also vary. Typically, the color gamut of a photo inkjet printer will not be as big as the gamut of your camera but will overlap that of the display. Here again, a professional color display will provide a better window on the colors being edited but won't always show a complete picture of what the final color print will look like. Soft proofing in Lightroom can help, because this allows you to see a modified preview filtered through the known profile of the printing paper you are using, but the limitations of the display mean it can't show you everything. But as long as you are editing in Lightroom, what can be printed in the raw original can be printed via Lightroom regardless of whether the display can show those colors or not. Obviously, the better the window you have to view those colors, the better the results will be, hence the importance of getting a good quality display to work with (see the diagram "Comparing Different Color Spaces" later in this chapter).

When you edit your images in Photoshop, the aim should be to preserve as much of the original color information as possible. This is why I recommend you configure ProPhoto RGB as the color space in the External Editing preferences (see Figure 2.9). ProPhoto RGB is an ultrawide gamut space, which, like the RGB space used in Lightroom, can easily encompass all the colors captured by your camera. By converting the raw files to ProPhoto RGB when you render a TIFF image, you preserve as much of the color information as possible when going from Lightroom to Photoshop and back again to Lightroom. If all the images you work on are going to originate from Lightroom, it is important you configure the Lightroom External Editing preferences appropriately, but it is essential to configure the Photoshop Color Settings correctly, too (see **Figure 2.13**). Here, I recommend setting the RGB working space to ProPhoto RGB and making sure you have Preserve Embedded Profiles selected in the Color Management Policies section.

ProPhoto RGB and its Lightroom variant are ideal spaces to work in, because they allow you to preserve as much color information as possible. Even with black-and-white images they can ensure better tonal rendition in the shadow areas when converting the image data to a print output space. It is important, though, to keep the editing in 16 bit throughout (which Lightroom does anyway).

ProPhoto RGB is not, however, a suitable space for distributing photos to others unless you are absolutely certain your recipients know how to handle profiled RGB images. If distributing photos for web use, you will definitely want to convert to sRGB when you export. This is because sRGB is a standardized RGB space for the web. When handing photos off to clients or photo labs, sRGB will always be a safe choice, but you might consider Adobe RGB as long as you are confident the recipients won't strip the embedded profile.

TIP

It does not matter too much if the RGB working space in the Photoshop Color Settings is set to something other than ProPhoto RGB. It is more important that you have the Color Management Policies set to Preserve Embedded Profiles and have ProPhoto RGB set as Color Space in the Lightroom External Editing preferences.

FIGURE 2.13 The Photoshop Color Settings, which can be accessed via the Edit menu. Shown is a custom setting that specifies ProPhoto RGB as the default RGB working edit space.

FIGURE 2.14 This portrait of Jeff Schewe is the photograph I used to compare the selection of different color spaces.

Color profile calibration

If the camera you are using is supported by Lightroom, there is no need to profile the camera, because there will already be Adobe Standard as well other manufacturer-based camera profiles to select from. It is possible to create a custom profile for your own camera, for which you will simply need an X-Rite ColorChecker target to photograph and the free Adobe DNG Profile Editor program. See the previous section "Calibration Settings" for more detail on these issues.

If you want accurate color, you must calibrate the display you are using. This can be done using a colorimeter. An emissive spectrophotometer can be useful if you intend to make your own custom print profiles as well, but you don't need to go to that expense if all you need to do is calibrate the display—a good colorimeter will do just fine. Just load the software that comes with the colorimeter and follow the onscreen instructions to measure and create a custom profile for your display.

It is also important to note, though, that the only effective way to judge the colors in an image in Lightroom is via the Develop module. The preview you see there is updated on the fly and provides the most accurate color preview, but at the expense of being slightly slower when you navigate from one image to the next. The previews you see elsewhere, such as in the Library module, are cached Adobe RGB JPEG previews, which are not as color-accurate but do offer the benefit of faster image navigation. The color differences will be most noticeable in the shadow areas, where the Library module Loupe view will be more likely to show signs of banding compared with the Develop module preview.

Printer ICC profiles should be available from the printer manufacturer either online or on a DVD that comes with the printer. Third-party print paper sellers may also provide ICC profiles ready for you to install and use. Failing that, you can arrange to have your own custom print profiles made by a profile providing company. They will ask you to print out a supplied color target (make sure you carefully follow the supplied print instructions) and send them a print, from which they will carry out the measurements and send you back a custom ICC profile. I find if you stick to using the regular paper media for which there are readily available canned profiles, you should get great results. In the early years the color output from inkjet printers could vary quite a bit from one machine to another. These days the results are far more consistent, which means the canned profiles should suit all printers that are the same make and model.

Windows systems allow 10-bit displays to show true 10-bit color, whereas on the latest Macintosh systems a 10-bit display depth is achieved through the use of dithering. Since many displays are in effect still 8-bit devices, this can sometimes lead to the perception of banding, when in fact the underlying image data does not necessarily have any banding at all and will print just fine.

Comparing different color spaces

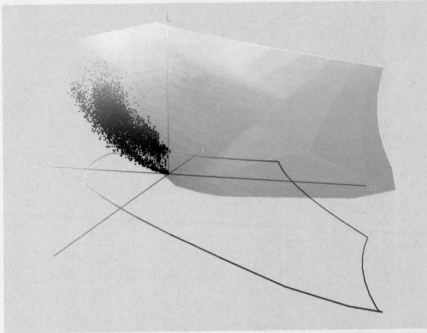

1 This 3D diagram shows the color gamut of a dark blue saturated photographic image (shown in **Figure 2.14**) plotted as dots overlaid with the color gamut of an iMac computer display, shown as a shaded shape. As you can see, most of the dots fall outside the gamut of the display. While an image like this may look OK on the display, what is seen is not a true representation of the colors actually contained in the sensor capture. These out-of-gamut colors have to be compressed in order to fit the limited gamut of the display.

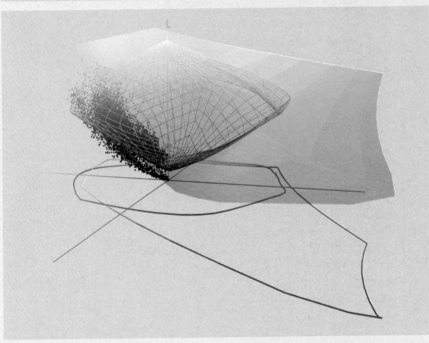

2 This diagram now includes an overlay showing the color gamut of an inkjet printer glossy paper output, represented here as a wire frame shape. Note how the display is unable to accurately show the out-of-gamut colors onscreen (because it is unable to reproduce them). However, when printing to this particular glossy paper the printer is actually capable of reproducing most of the colors contained in the capture, but not all. Those that are out of gamut still have to be mapped to the nearest in-gamut equivalent. The colors in the actual file are still printable, you just can't see the complete picture on the screen even though the display may be calibrated.

3 Let's now consider the relationship between the color gamut of the image, the display, and the RGB work space. In this diagram the image is plotted as dots again with the color gamut of the Mac display represented here as a wire frame shape. This is overlaid by the ProPhoto RGB space represented as a shaded shape. Once again you can see how the color gamut of the image falls outside the gamut of the display, but the ultrawide gamut of the ProPhoto RGB space (on which the Lightroom edit space is based) is sufficient to contain both.

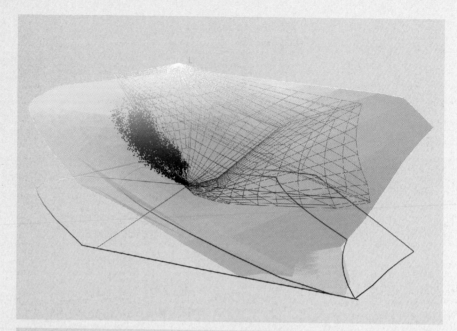

4 Likewise, when you compare the color gamut of the image with that of the print output (represented here as a wire frame shape), the color gamut of ProPhoto RGB is able to contain everything. Although ProPhoto RGB may seem excessively large, its size ensures that when editing in Lightroom and Photoshop you have the headroom to manage colors from input to edit to output without incurring any clipping. Also, the default 16-bit editing in Lightroom ensures ultimate accuracy when converting data from one color space to another.

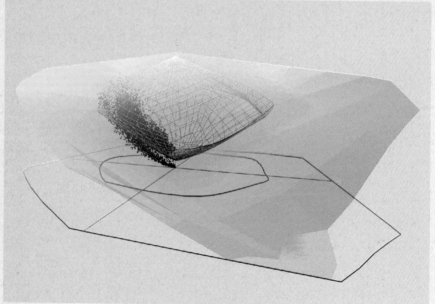

PRINT OUTPUT

Both Photoshop and Lightroom are capable of making high-quality prints, but personally, I much prefer to use Lightroom. This is because there are a number of advantages to printing in Lightroom. It provides an easy-to-access soft proofing mechanism with which to preview files prior to printing, automatic print sharpening is available within the program, custom settings can be saved within a print template setting, and draft-mode printing provides a quick and easy way to generate contact sheet prints.

FIGURE 2.15 Checking the Soft Proofing option in the Develop module toolbar enables a soft proof preview, reveals the Proof Settings options, and makes the Histogram panel become the Soft Proofing panel.

NOTE

Lightroom provides two rendering intent options: Perceptual and
Relative Colorimetric. Both are
suitable for photographic printing.
You can read up about the differences between the two if you
like. But at the end of the day, the
choice is subjective. Use the soft
proofing to gauge which looks
best to you.

NOTE

You can use the Photo ⇨ Create
Virtual Copy command to create a
virtual copy of the original image.
This is not an actual duplicate, but
rather a settings copy with a separate preview.

Soft proof checking

The Develop module has a Soft Proofing option in the Toolbar (**Figure 2.15**). When this is checked, the image canvas changes from gray to white and the Histogram panel becomes the Soft Proofing panel, where you can use the Proof Settings section to select the desired printer profile and rendering intent. The available profiles will be determined by those that you have selected from the Print module Print Job panel (see the instructions in **Figure 2.16**). When you select a print profile, the preview display changes to show an onscreen preview of how the image is likely to print using the selected profile and rendering intent. Each time you select a new profile, the soft proof preview will adapt accordingly. You can now make further Develop module edits filtered via the print output preview, which in turn will prompt you to create a new soft proof copy (a virtual copy) separate from the master version. Now, the extent to which you can preview the actual colors will be determined by the limits of the color gamut of the display—there may be colors you can't see that will be printable. This might suggest that soft proofing is nonsense, but it does also preview changes to the luminance, in particular the paper white and black ink output, which means you can certainly use a soft proofed display to compensate for changes in contrast.

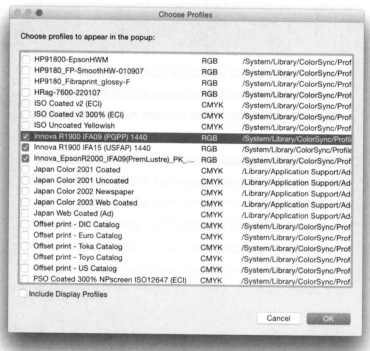

FIGURE 2.16 Click on the profile menu in the Lightroom Print module Print Job panel and select Other to open the system dialog shown here, where you can select the print profiles you specifically wish to see appear when you mouse down on this menu.

PRINT MODULE SETTINGS

When you are ready to print, switch to the Print module (**Figure 2.17**), where you can use the panels on the right to adjust the layout. In the Color Management section of the Print Job panel, you should make sure the profile selected matches that selected at the soft proofing stage (thereby disabling the Managed by Printer option) and also ensure the rendering intent matches as well. The Print Sharpening menu offers three choices: Low, Standard and High. I usually recommend Standard. Below that select the media type: Glossy or Matte. These options determine how much behind-the-scenes sharpening is automatically applied to the print file. You won't see any change in the appearance of the screen image. It simply ensures the print looks as sharp as what you see on the display. The Print Adjustment section can be used to apply Brightness and Contrast compensation to the final print output. This, too, happens behind the scenes and is not reflected in the display preview. Basically, if despite everything you do in a color-managed workflow, the prints appear to be darker or flatter than what you see on the computer, you can compensate using these controls.

FIGURE 2.17 The Print module with the Print Job panel options.

Page Setup and Print Settings (Macintosh)

1 The Macintosh Print Module has two buttons in the bottom-left section: Page Setup and Print Settings. I clicked on the Page Setup button first. Shown here is the Macintosh operating system Page Setup dialog showing the options for an Epson R2000 printer. In the Paper Size section, I selected A3+ as the desired paper size, selected Landscape for the print orientation, and clicked OK to save.

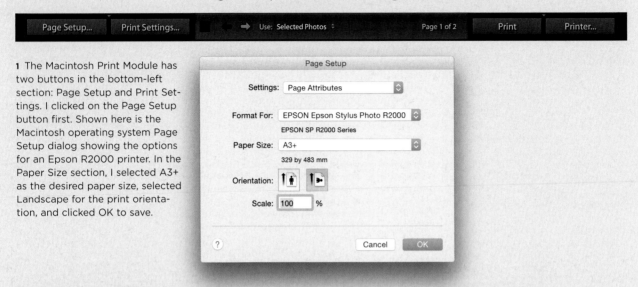

2 Next, I clicked on the Print Settings button, which again showed the options for the Epson R2000 printer. I selected the Print Settings options (circled) and chose the intended media type (Epson Premium Glossy). Incidentally, with the Mac operating system, the Epson driver automatically disables the color management options when anything other than Managed by Printer is selected in the Lightroom Print Job panel Color Management section. Lastly, I selected the highest print quality option and clicked the Save button at the bottom to return to Lightroom.

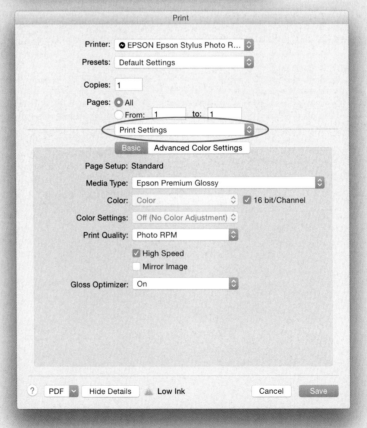

Page Setup and Print Settings (PC)

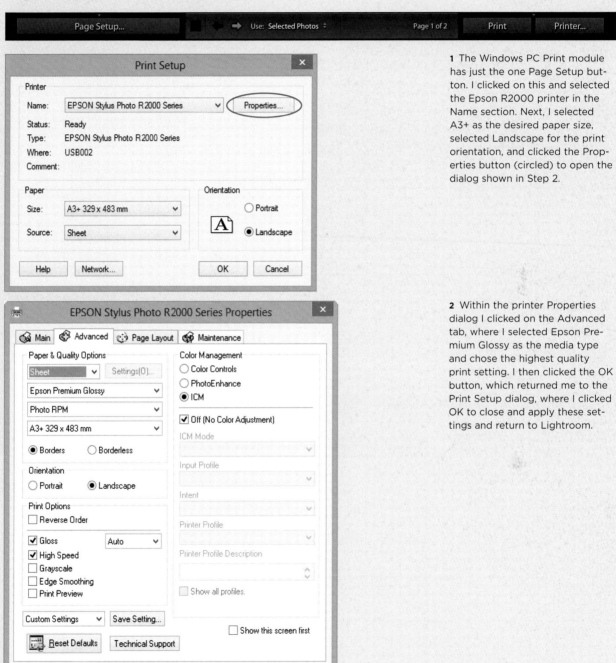

1 The Windows PC Print module has just the one Page Setup button. I clicked on this and selected the Epson R2000 printer in the Name section. Next, I selected A3+ as the desired paper size, selected Landscape for the print orientation, and clicked the Properties button (circled) to open the dialog shown in Step 2.

2 Within the printer Properties dialog I clicked on the Advanced tab, where I selected Epson Premium Glossy as the media type and chose the highest quality print setting. I then clicked the OK button, which returned me to the Print Setup dialog, where I clicked OK to close and apply these settings and return to Lightroom.

Final Print system Print dialog settings (Mac & PC)

1 When you click on the Printer button in the Print module, this once again opens the system Print dialog, where, on a Macintosh computer you need to double-check that the Presets menu says Default Settings (circled). If it doesn't, the print media settings will most likely be incorrect. You can, if you like, quickly confirm the settings are right by selecting Print Settings from the menu below and check that the settings displayed match those entered earlier when you first established them.

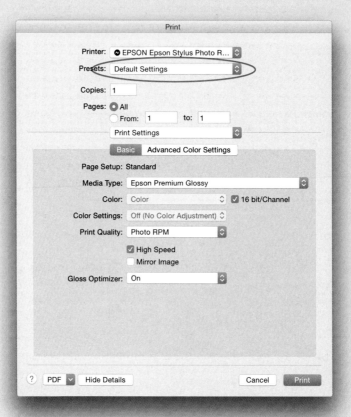

2 On a Windows PC computer, clicking the Printer... button opens the Windows system Print dialog shown here, where the print settings should also remain unchanged since you established these earlier. You can confirm that is the case by clicking on the Properties... button and checking the print settings are the same and you don't have a custom preset print setting selected.

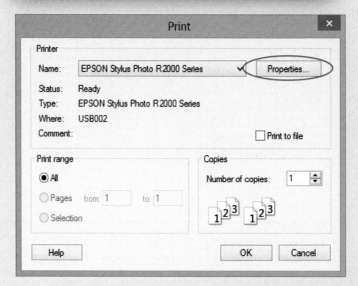

Saving the print settings as a preset

Once you have configured the settings for a particular print layout, it is a good idea to save these as a print preset via the Template Browser panel in the Print module (see **Figure 2.18**). The great thing about Lightroom is that once you have chosen all your desired settings in the Print module, you can save everything as a single preset. The Print template settings will include the selected printer, the paper size, orientation and media type, the print media type, the quality settings, and finally, the print layout adjustment settings established in the Layout Style, Image Settings, Layout Guides, Page, and Print Job panels (including the color profile, sharpening, and print adjustment). The next time you need to make a similar type of print using the same printer and media, you just need to select the desired print template and click the Print or Printer buttons. You will then be guaranteed the print result will match the settings you configured previously exactly.

Of course, it is likely you will want to vary the layout and other settings slightly when making future prints. So once you have created a template that works for a particular printer, you can select the current template, adjust the Print module settings as required, and save as a new print template. You will notice that if you select a print template and alter the Print module settings in any way, the existing print template appears unhighlighted. If you wish to revise the settings and update a current template, right mouse-click on the print template name and select Update with Current Settings from the contextual menu (see **Figure 2.19**). So, if you save a print template and later realize it needs revision, you can use the contextual menu to do this.

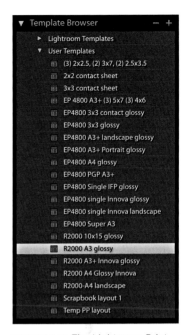

FIGURE 2.18 The Lightroom Print module Template Browser panel.

ARCHIVING YOUR WORK

It is vital that you employ a backup strategy for your data. At the very least you should periodically back up the data from the computer's drive to a backup drive. Ideally, you want to have two backup drives so that you are able to switch backups and keep the second backup off-site somewhere. As you add more drives to store data, you'll need to purchase extra backup drives. This backup system is known as Just a Bunch of Disks, or JBOD, and is effective and relatively easy to implement. All you need is the software to manage the backup copying and the knowhow to connect the external drives. On the Macintosh system I use a program called Carbon Copy Cloner to manage the backup process. This can be configured so that the program analyzes what is on the source and destination disks and copies only the files that are missing on the destination or copies and overwrites the files that have been modified since the last backup. With Carbon Copy Cloner (CCC) you can also create bootable backups. Should your main system disk go down, you can use a CCC bootable copy drive to reboot from. Therefore in an emergency you can be up and running again in a matter of minutes. For PC users, Retrospect is a very popular and also provides bootable disk support.

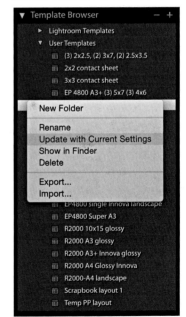

FIGURE 2.19 The Lightroom Print module Template Browser panel showing the contextual menu.

WHERE ARE YOUR FILES ARCHIVED?

It is important to understand that when you import files into Lightroom you are copying the files to a specific, designated folder location, just as you would if you copied the files directly from the card. The Lightroom catalog references the files and everything that is done to them. Consequently, you need to safeguard the files you import just as you would do normally. You don't want to delete them thinking they are somehow stored inside the Lightroom catalog itself. The Lightroom catalog file is therefore a very important document that you want to back up regularly and keep safe.

STORAGE

Hard disk drives are the cheapest form of high-capacity storage you can buy. Because these are mechanical devices they will eventually wear out after a few years of heavy use. Hence it's a wise precaution to upgrade and replace all your hard disk drives every few years, especially if you're running a business. Usually you will find the prices have come tumbling down and you can purchase drives with double the capacity for the same price as your old drives. For optimum performance you shouldn't allow hard disk drives to reach full capacity. As you store more data on the drive, the performance will diminish as you get close to 85 percent full capacity. This is because the hard disk drive actuator arm is having to do a lot more work reading from and searching for free sectors on the disk to write to, resulting in slower read-write speeds. Solid State Drives (or SSDs) have no moving parts and are popular because they offer much faster read-write speeds compared to regular hard disk drives, but these are more expensive, of course. Ideally, you should use an SSD as your main boot drive and to run the operating system and applications. This will greatly speed the time it takes to load from startup and launch all your applications. You can partition an SSD to create a separate scratch disk for Photoshop use. Now, with conventional hard drives the scratch partition had to be on a separate hard drive (such as a RAID 0 for extra speed). Because there are no mechanical parts in an SSD and it is faster, it is fine to create a second partition of, say, 40GB and use this for scratch. However, SSDs can fail just as easily as conventional hard drives, so you have to be equally vigilant about maintaining backups and replacing your SSDs every few years.

Lightroom will run faster if the Lightroom catalog folder is located on an SSD. While the catalog file is likely to be only a few GB in size, the Previews file may be several hundred GB, plus you may choose to generate smart previews each time you import, which can also increase the size of the Lightroom folder contents. It all depends on how many photographs you intend to manage in Lightroom, but for a large image catalog the Lightroom catalog folder might need about 250 to 500 GB of disk storage space. Therefore, if you want to store the catalog on an SSD, you might want to consider an external SSD with a fast connection such as USB 3.

One advantage of doing this is that it makes it easier to transfer your catalog between two computers, especially if you choose to generate smart previews of your files as they are imported. Again, do consider what might happen if you were to lose the disk containing the catalog, and always have up-to-date offline backups.

FILE FORMATS

While different types of storage media have come and gone over the last two decades, the TIFF and JPEG formats have remained a constant. TIFF in particular is a versatile format for archiving your master retouched images. The current TIFF 6 specification has been around since 1992. Just about every image-editing program can read TIFF format files, although you should be wary of using some of the compression options when saving as a TIFF because ZIP and JPEG compression are not supported by older TIFF readers. Raw files include hundreds of different types, which are all undocumented, proprietary raw formats. Each raw file format is therefore dependent on the user having the necessary proprietary raw software to open them. Although Adobe Camera Raw/Lightroom and other third-party programs provide support for these raw file formats, these programs are in turn dependent on continued developer and operating system support to guarantee that an undocumented raw file created today can be read in say, 10, 50, or 100 years' time.

DNG format

Adobe's solution to the above problem is the DNG raw file format. This can be used to archive any of the 500-plus types of raw files that are currently supported in Lightroom in a standardized format, which can be read by a number of raw processing programs including, of course, Lightroom and Camera Raw. You will notice that whenever you import files into Lightroom, you have the option to convert to DNG. You can also do this by making a selection of photos in the Library module and choosing Library ➾ Convert Photos to DNG. The only proviso is that the photos you import or select are in a raw format Lightroom recognizes. Some cameras even give you the option to capture DNG files.

   The DNG format was originally designed with raw files in mind, but you can also use it to archive JPEGs, and here's why. Lightroom allows you to import both raw and JPEG image files and edit them using the Lightroom Develop controls. Therefore, you can have JPEG master images to which Lightroom Develop adjustments have been applied. If you want to export your edited JPEGs and preserve the settings so they remain editable, the best way to do this is by exporting as DNG. That way others can see your JPEGs with the Lightroom edits as fully adjustable settings (providing they are using Lightroom or Camera Raw). At the same time, saving as a DNG file saves a Lightroom adjusted preview, so when it's viewed in any third-party, DNG-aware program, the correct preview is seen, even if it doesn't have the same edit controls as Lightroom or Camera Raw.

NOTE

Smart previews can be created at the time of import or created manually by making a selection of photos and choosing Library ➾ Previews ➾ Build Smart Previews. Smart previews are lightweight versions of the master images that can be used in place of the original raw files throughout Lightroom. They are effectively lossy DNG versions of the original masters resized to 2,560 pixels along the longest edge and stored in a single archive file inside the Lightroom catalog folder.

The DNG format is an open standard, which means the file format specification (which is based on the TIFF file format) is freely available to all third-party developers. A number of programs other than Lightroom and Photoshop are able to read from and write to DNG files, which supports the case for DNG as an archive format that meets the criteria for long-term file preservation that will enable future generations to access and read the DNG raw data. This should hold true even if Adobe isn't always going to be around, in the same way TIFF files look set to be readable for the foreseeable future.

For now, there is no imminent need to convert to DNG since undocumented raw formats are still widely read. For the long term, legitimate concerns come into play. Major operating system updates have been known to make older operating systems and the software that runs on them obsolete within a matter of a few years. Therefore, continued support for undocumented file formats is directly dependent on future support of those applications. It is likely Adobe will be around 10 years from now, but photographers should really be asking themselves, what will happen in 50 or 100 years' time? The DNG format also contains a checksum validation feature, which can be used to spot corrupted DNG files. This will be a useful feature for archivists to check on the condition of archived files. The DNG format allows you to enable Fast Load Data, which stores a standard-size preview in the DNG file. This enables faster loading when opening an image in Camera Raw or Lightroom. Finally, the DNG spec allows for image tiling, which can speed up file data read times with multicore processors compared with reading a continuous compressed raw file, which can be read by only one processor core at a time.

Converting to DNG has its downsides, most notably, the added time it takes to convert raw files to DNG. You do lose the ability to process DNG files using the manufacturer's dedicated raw processing software, unless you choose to embed the original raw inside the DNG (which can double the file size because you will be storing two raw files in one container). If you save edit changes to the DNG files, this will slow down the backup process because the backup software will have to copy the complete DNGs instead of just the XMP sidecar files that otherwise accompany the proprietary raw images. Personally, I believe it is better to let the catalog file store the metadata edits rather than constantly overwrite the files referenced by the catalog. If you are in the habit of saving metadata edits to the files themselves as well, this is an important consideration, but you need to ask yourself, "In an emergency, when I need to restore all my metadata edits, which is going to be the most up-to-date? The metadata stored in the files, or the metadata stored in the catalog?"

3

TONE AND COLOR CORRECTIONS

BASIC ADJUSTMENTS TO OPTIMIZE YOUR IMAGES

TONE RANGE

A raw file should give you plenty of scope to adjust the tones any way you want, especially since the sensors in recent cameras are now better than ever and can capture a wide range of tones. Early camera sensors had a more limited dynamic range, which meant it was absolutely critical to get the exposure right (as it was when shooting with transparency film). You have a little more latitude now with the capture exposure settings and can manipulate the detail in the shadows and highlights with much greater ease.

When preparing a digital image, the tone and color editing is the most important step of all. What you do at the tone and color edit stage is key to the success of everything else you might do to an image, whether it is intended for print, for the screen, or for use as an element in another photograph. It is therefore necessary to have a good grasp of how best to optimize your images in Lightroom and why (most of the time) it is important to maximize the detail in the shadow and highlight areas. It's also good to understand how to control the color and the color-editing tools. All these can be found in the Develop module, where the Basic panel is the best place to make the initial tone and color edits.

Throughout this chapter I will guide you through the essential steps to adjust your images, where the approach I recommend is to first adjust the tone and color to create an optimized version and use this as the starting point for further, secondary edit adjustments.

LEVELS/EXPOSURE ADJUSTMENTS

Any type of image adjustment involves altering the pixel values from their original settings. This always causes some loss of image information, because it involves compressing some of the levels closer together and, at the same time, stretching others farther apart. This is the trade-off you make when you modify an image. If you do nothing to alter an image, a rendered pixel output will preserve all the tonal and color detail of the original. If you edit the tones and colors in any way, the rendered image may be more pleasing to look at but will nonetheless be a degraded derivative. Of course, anything you do in Lightroom is stored as instructional edits, and the master files are left untouched. But the edits you apply in Lightroom do have a bearing on the final integrity of the image when it is output as a TIFF, PSD, or JPEG rendered file.

If the master image data you are editing is a raw file, which contains, say, several thousand levels of data per channel, that is a lot of levels of information to be playing with. The fact that the image adjustments you apply may reduce the number of potential levels by half is not such a big deal. Yes, the output image will be degraded, but in most cases enough levels will remain so that the quality of the print output will not be compromised. It is only when you apply major edits to the dark shadow areas that you may see signs of banding or posterization. This is because there will be fewer levels to play with in the shadows.

In **Figure 3.1**, the top image shows a normally exposed photograph, where the Histogram panel indicates that this image has a fairly even, broad range of tones that slope up from the darkest shadow point to the quarter tones, midtones, and three-quarter tones, before sloping down to the brightest highlight point. The middle version shows what happens to the image and histogram when you apply a darkening Levels image adjustment. Notice how this causes the shadow-to-midtone levels to compress and the midtone-to-highlight levels to stretch farther apart. This is because the dark tones have become compressed. Consequently, there is less tonal separation in these areas and the shadows have become flatter in contrast. Meanwhile, the tone contrast has increased in the midtone-to-highlight levels. In the bottom version, a lightening Levels adjustment was applied. In this example, the shadow levels were stretched farther apart and the midtone-to-highlight tones became more compressed. It is noticeable how the midtone-to-highlight tones now have less tonal separation and are lacking in contrast.

What these examples demonstrate is that after you have applied an image adjustment, the many levels of tone information that exist in the original will eventually be aggregated down to a smaller number of levels. Where the tones are expanded, gaps will appear between the levels. Where the tones are compressed, many of the tone levels will end up sharing the same levels value. Whether you darken, lighten, add contrast, or decrease the contrast, you always lose some levels.

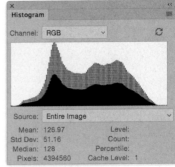

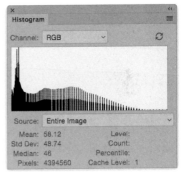

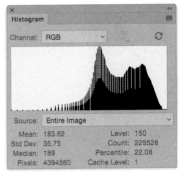

FIGURE 3.1 A comparison of lightening and darkening Levels adjustments on an image.

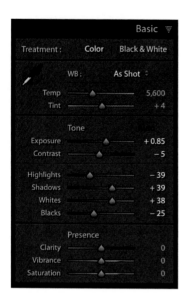

FIGURE 3.2 The Basic panel featuring the Tone controls.

LIGHTROOM BASIC PANEL ADJUSTMENTS

The majority of the tone and color editing can be carried out using the Develop module's Basic panel (**Figure 3.2**). The other panels are important, too, but the Basic panel is where you want to get started and do most of the "heavy lifting." This is because it gives you a greater degree of control over the way the levels are manipulated. The Basic panel Tone section features six sliders: Exposure, Contrast, Highlights, Shadows, Whites, and Blacks. It does not necessarily matter in which order you adjust these, although it is usually best to apply them in the order they are presented.

EXPOSURE

Adjusting the Exposure slider is similar to adjusting the input Gamma slider in the Photoshop Levels dialog, although the Exposure slider in Lightroom is actually a little more sophisticated than that. This is because the Exposure slider is both a midtone brightness and highlight-clipping adjustment rolled into one. As you drag the slider to the right, this increases the brightness of an image, and as you further increase the brightness, the white clipping point will be preserved. As you approach the point where the highlights might become clipped, the brightening adjustment smoothly ramps off toward the highlight end, which helps preserve detail in the highlight areas. Such Exposure adjustments should result in smoother highlights with reduced color shifts. Essentially, the Exposure slider's response correlates quite well with the way film behaved when you adjusted the camera exposure, but the Exposure slider's behavior and responsiveness also depends on the image content. This means you can safely lighten an image without fear of causing unwanted clipping in the highlights, as long as you aren't deliberately overbrightening it. If you overbrighten an image with the Exposure slider, some highlight clipping may occur.

Similarly, you can drag to the left to darken photos that appear overexposed and restore highlight detail that at first might appear to be missing. How much you can recover will all depend on the sensor. You should certainly be able to recover as much as one stop of overexposure and with some cameras even more, but there are limits. For example, when I have shot using the Hasselblad H4D back, I find there is limited headroom to prevent highlight clipping on overexposed captures (even with the aid of the Highlights slider, which I discuss later).

In most instances, it is best to combine an Exposure adjustment with the other tone sliders in order to have complete control over the final tone appearance. First, adjust using Exposure to get the image brightness looking roughly right. Then, as you adjust the other tone sliders, the midpoint brightness value shouldn't shift too much. You can, if you wish, choose to make a further fine-tuning adjustment with the Exposure slider after you have adjusted the remaining sliders.

Lightening an underexposed image

Good image editing is often about making the final image as representative as possible of what you saw at the time the photograph was taken. For various reasons, your photographs won't always look exactly how you expected them to. In this instance, the original was underexposed by about a stop, so I clearly needed to lighten the image using the Exposure slider. However, as I adjusted the Exposure setting I had to pay careful attention to the shadow detail because there were fewer levels to play with, and dramatically lightening the image would risk revealing more shadow noise. When you compensate for an underexposed image such as this, it is also harder to set the optimum clipping points and, at the same time, preserve a delicate balance in the shadow contrast. You will notice that in the initial step I chose to set the Contrast slider to -47. This flattened the global contrast to produce a balanced distribution of tones, where I was then able to use the extended Tone Curve controls (in Step 3) to manipulate and improve upon the adjusted base-level contrast.

Photograph: © Farid Sani

1 This shows the before version of a photograph taken by Farid Sani. As you can see, it was underexposed. The following steps show how I was able to lighten the image and improve the contrast.

2 I began by dealing with the biggest problem first, which was to lighten the image and rescue the shadow detail. I did this by going to the Basic panel, where I applied the adjustments shown here to lighten Exposure, lighten Shadows, and fine-tune Whites and Blacks clipping points. The aim here was to achieve a full tone contrast that could be further manipulated using the Tone Curve panel.

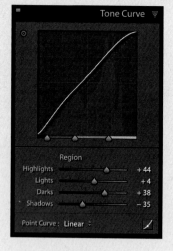

3 I then selected the Graduated Filter tool and added a darkening gradient to the top half of the photograph. I went to the Tone Curve panel and adjusted the slider controls to carefully adjust the contrast at the Shadows and Highlight ends of the curve. I refined the Tone Curve adjustment with the Zone Range sliders just beneath the tone curve.

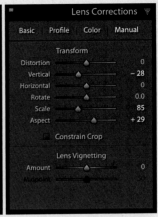

Photograph © Farid Sani

4 After that, I selected the Lens Corrections panel, where I applied a profiled lens correction and checked the Remove Color Aberration box. Lastly, I adjusted the Manual Transform sliders to adjust the vertical distortion and used the Crop Overlay tool to crop the image more tightly to a square format. This made the boab trees very much the center of focus in this final composition.

Photoshop Curves versus Lightroom Shadows adjustments

1 Here is a low-key photograph that I edited in Lightroom using the Basic panel. In this step, the Shadows slider (circled) was set to zero.

2 I then chose Photo ⇨ Edit in ⇨ Photoshop, where I added a Curves adjustment layer and applied the Curves adjustment shown below to lighten the shadows. Note how I anchored the highlight tone section of the curve.

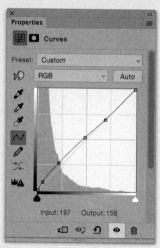

3 I then returned to Lightroom and applied a +100 Shadows adjustment to the original master image to lighten the shadow tone areas.

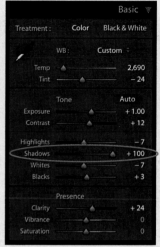

4 Here you can see a comparison of the two types of image adjustment. On the left you can see the Photoshop Curves adjusted version (applied using the Normal blend mode) and on the right is the Lightroom Shadows adjusted version. When I applied the Photoshop Curves adjustment, I tried to match as closely as possible the Lightroom Shadows adjusted version. As you can see, the Photoshop Curves adjustment lightens, but in doing so flattens the contrast in the shadow-to-midtone areas. However, the Lightroom Shadows adjusted version lightens, but at the same time retains more contrast in the shadow-to-midtone areas.

There is a subtle difference between Photoshop Curves and
Lightroom Contrast adjustments.
Lightroom Contrast and Tone
Curve adjustments are hue-locked.
If you compare a contrast-increasing Photoshop Curves adjustment
with a similar adjustment carried
out in Lightroom using the Basic
panel Contrast slider or Tone
Curve panel, you will discover that
the Photoshop image pixel values
will shift in luminance, saturation,
and hue, whereas when you apply
a Lightroom contrast adjustment,
the hue values will be locked and
there will be no hue shifts.

CONTRAST

The Contrast slider in Lightroom can be used to increase or decrease the global contrast. Lightroom Basic panel Contrast adjustments are similar to those that can be achieved using the Tone Curve panel in Lightroom or the Curves adjustment in Photoshop, where an S-shaped curve will increase the image contrast. As you heighten the contrast in Lightroom or Photoshop, you will notice how the saturation also increases (see **Figure 3.3**). In Photoshop you can lock the hue and saturation by setting the Curves adjustment layer blend mode to Luminosity. This can sometimes be a desirable thing to do when applying localized contrast-increasing adjustments. On the whole, photographers like to see the saturation increase as they boost the contrast. Consequently, there is no saturation lock in Lightroom for the Basic panel Contrast slider and Tone Curve panel.

The Contrast slider behavior does adapt slightly according to the image content based on which tones predominate in the image you are editing. With dark photos, the midpoint for the contrast adjustment is offset slightly toward the shadows, and with high-key images, the midpoint is offset slightly toward the highlights. For photo-graphs that require a contrast adjustment, it is best to adjust the Basic panel Contrast slider first. You can, if you wish, follow this with a fine-tuning adjustment using the Tone Curve panel controls.

FIGURE 3.3 A comparison of a zero Contrast setting (left) and a +100 Contrast adjust-ment (right), carried out using the Lightroom Basic panel Contrast slider.

HIGHLIGHTS AND SHADOWS

The Highlights and Shadows sliders can be used to lighten or darken. A negative Highlights adjustment darkens the highlight tones extending slightly beyond the midtone areas. Likewise, a positive Shadows adjustment will lighten the shadow tones (also extending slightly beyond the midtone areas). The effect each of these sliders has on the tones in an image is basically symmetrical. For instance, when processing an image with a wide dynamic range, you will usually want to apply a negative Highlights adjustment combined with a positive Shadows adjustment.

There are also good reasons why you might want to drag these sliders in opposite directions. For example, a positive Highlights adjustment can be used to deliberately compress highlight tonal detail and soften the highlight tones. Meanwhile, a negative Shadows adjustment can be used to compress the shadow tones—you can remove detail in a dark background by making the dark tones go darker.

These two sliders are really powerful and have an important role to play when balancing the tones in an image because they give you independent tone control of the highlight and shadow areas. When they are used with restraint, the effect these sliders can have is quite subtle, but as you extend the values beyond plus or minus 50, you may start to see noticeable halos appearing around the edges of high contrast. This can sometimes result in what looks like a fake HDR-type effect, especially if you combine a -100 Highlights adjustment with a +100 Shadows adjustment. This won't always happen, though. When processing HDR-merged master images, you will often need to push these two sliders to their extremes and can do so without generating ugly halos. However, with regular images the results can look rather artificial if you overdo it.

WHITES AND BLACKS

The Whites and Blacks sliders are fine-tuning controls that can be used to set the clipping points for the white point and black point in an image. I usually adjust these two sliders last. I will adjust the White slider so that the brightest (nonspecular) highlight tones are just starting to clip and then ease off slightly to ensure these tones are preserved when going to print. With the Blacks slider, I will set this to the point where the blackest blacks just start to clip. When making these adjustments, you can hold down the a key as you do so to see a threshold clipping preview display, which can help guide you in estimating the clipping points. The Blacks slider is also adaptive. This means that when editing a soft contrast image, such as a high-key, misty landscape, the Blacks slider adapts to extend the range controlled by the Blacks slider at the expense of losing some precision.

How to deliberately lose highlight detail

This photograph of a clump of trees surrounded by empty common was shot one winter's morning as the snow was falling. My plan was to create a black-and-white photograph where the trees were isolated in a sea of white. Here, I shot a sequence of photos and merged these into a single panorama. This allowed me to extend the angle of view and create a high-resolution image. The result was a high-key photograph where the focus was kept on the trees. Some people might like to bleach the highlights out even more to create an extreme high-contrast look. However, with this particular image I didn't want to distort the tone range too much.

1 To create this image, I shot five photographs with the camera oriented in portrait mode so that I could create a single panorama image. I selected the photos in Lightroom and chose Photo ⇨ Photo Merge ⇨ Panorama.

2 This opened the Panorama Merge Preview dialog, where I manually selected the Cylindrical projection option (Cylindrical is usually the best option when merging a single row of images). I then clicked the Merge button.

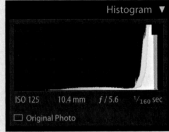

3 This generated a merged panorama that was saved as a DNG file and automatically added to the Lightroom catalog. The Histogram panel also confirmed that the merged photo lacked contrast.

4 Next, I selected the Crop Overlay tool in the Develop module and cropped the image to trim the outside areas so that the clump of trees was centered in the frame.

5 I then applied some tone adjustments via the Basic panel in the Develop module, where I increased Exposure to +0.85 and set Contrast to +16. To lighten the overall image, I set Highlights to +75, which flattened the contrast in the highlight regions. This caused the brightest highlights to clip slightly just behind the trees where the sky was brightest. I also went to the Split Toning panel and added a cooling split-tone effect to enhance the wintry feel in this photo.

6 I then added a Graduated FIlter adjustment to the bottom section of the photograph, where I also applied a positive Highlights adjustment. I combined this with a positive Clarity adjustment to bring out more detail in the grass that was poking through the snow.

7 Next, I applied a Radial Filter adjustment that was applied to the outer areas (shaded here with a red overlay). With this adjustment I increased Exposure slightly and also reduced the Contrast setting.

8 I then duplicated the Radial Filter adjustment (you can do this by right-clicking on an existing localized adjustment button and selecting Duplicate) and checked the Inverse Mask button (circled right). I set Exposure to -0.29 and increased Contrast to +31 and Clarity to +45. The intention here was to add more contrast and darken the shadows in the trees.

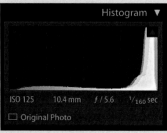

9 Here is the final edited version. The Histogram panel shows how the tone range is now extended more fully, where the shadows were just starting to clip. At the highlight end, you will notice how the highlights are much more clipped compared with the histogram shown in Step 3. You don't always want to clip the highlights so severely, but there are times when it is appropriate to do so. For example, where you have an image that has what are known as specular highlights (such as light reflecting off a shiny surface), these should be hard-clipped. With an image like this, the area clipped is the white sky. Even though there might have been some cloud detail to recover, in this instance the objective was to interpret the photograph as a stark-white snow scene, so clipping the whites created a greater degree of contrast with the trees.

AUTO TONE ADJUSTMENTS

If you are unsure how to adjust the sliders, you can click on the Auto button (circled in **Figure 3.4**) to apply an Auto adjustment based on a Lightroom analysis of the image. You will find that an Auto adjustment mostly automatically sets just the Exposure, Contrast, and Whites and Blacks sliders. But sometimes it will set the Highlights and Shadows sliders as well. Auto Tone adjustments can work well with certain types of subjects and produce an instant improved look. With photographs that have been shot under controlled lighting conditions, I generally find the results look worse. In any case, it does not do any harm to start by clicking on the Auto button to see if you like the look this gives you or not. An Auto Tone adjustment can be undone by double-clicking the Tone button next to Auto.

Individual Auto Tone adjustments

You can use s plus a double-click to independently set the Tone sliders. If you s double-click the Exposure, Contrast, Highlights, or Shadows sliders, this sets the individual sliders to the same setting as if you had clicked the Auto button. However, if you s double-click the Whites and Blacks sliders, Lightroom analyzes the image and computes the Whites or Blacks value needed to just begin to clip, which isn't quite the same as applying a standard Auto Tone adjustment. This is because the Auto adjustment is recalculated based on all other adjustment settings that may have been applied. So, if you manually alter the Exposure, Contrast, Highlights, or Shadows sliders, or crop the image, s double-clicking the Whites and Blacks sliders will yield an updated result.

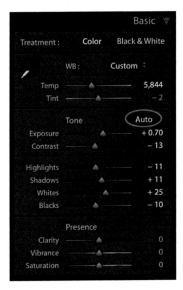

FIGURE 3.4 An example of an Auto Tone adjustment.

HARD-CLIPPING THE SHADOWS

Now let's look at an example of where you might want to clip the blacks in an image. With most photographs you want to set the shadow clipping point so that the shadows just begin to clip. You can check the clipping by holding down the a key as you adjust the Blacks slider. This shows a threshold clipping preview (like the one shown in **Figure 3.5**), which will help you judge how best to set the Blacks slider.

The following example shows a photograph that was taken from beneath a section of the Chicago L train. Here, I wanted to show how deliberately hard-clipping the shadows can create a dark mood. It can be used when editing photographs shot against a dark background, or, as in the following example, to create graphic shadows. For example, if you are photographing at a time when the sun is high in the sky, you either want to fill in the shadows or enhance them. If you are photographing cityscape shots, you'll find the following approach works well if you want to make the shadows go completely black. The result is similar to the printing technique favored by photographers such as Ralph Gibson and Bill Brandt.

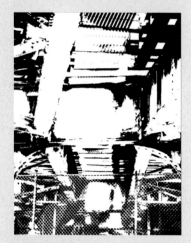

FIGURE 3.5 An example of a Shadows threshold mode clipping preview in Lightroom.

1 This shows the raw photo without any tone adjustments. Looking at the Histogram panel, you can see there is a nice even distribution of tones where the shadows are only just starting to clip.

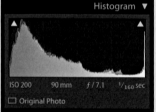

2 In this step, I set the Contrast slider to +80. This resulted in a loss of highlight detail, which I overcame by setting the Highlights slider to -60. The contrast boost also caused the shadows to go darker. Setting the Shadows slider to -50 made them go even darker still.

3 I then fine-tuned the clipping points. Here, I set the Whites slider to +20 and set the Blacks slider to -60. The Shadows adjustment combined with the Blacks adjustment ensured I would get extra-deep shadows.

4 In the Presence section of the Basic panel, I set the Clarity to +50 to boost the midtone contrast. This adjustment enhanced the gritty texture of the metal. I then applied a negative Vibrance adjustment to desaturate the colors slightly.

5 Having applied the main tone adjustments, I noticed how this created a hot spot in the middle of the picture. To address this, I selected the Radial Filter and added a negative Highlights adjustment to this area.

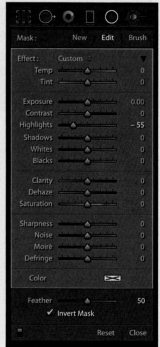

6 Here, you can see the final version where I added a gentle Split Toning adjustment to add a slight sepia color cast to the photograph. In the Histogram panel you can see how (compared with the original histogram) the highlights are no longer quite so clipped, but there is a lot of hard clipping at the shadow end.

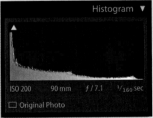

FIGURE 3.6 An example of a Highlights threshold mode clipping preview in Lightroom.

SETTING THE WHITES AND BLACKS IN A HIGH-KEY IMAGE

When photographing a high-key scene, such as the one featured here, you have to be careful to get the exposure right. If you use a standard, automatic mode, the camera will almost certainly underexpose your captures. In this instance, I used the camera meter more as a guide and varied the exposure around two-thirds to a stop above what the camera was telling me. Even so, I could probably have safely overexposed even further. With this photograph it was necessary to mainly use the Whites and Blacks sliders to expand the tonal range. When setting the highlights, you can hold down the [Alt] key as you drag the Whites slider to see a highlights threshold mode clipping preview (see **Figure 3.6**) and use this to help determine at which point it is safe to set the highlight clipping point so that the important highlights are not clipped. As I explained earlier, the Blacks slider in Lightroom is adaptive, which means the Blacks slider has the ability to adapt to extend the range controlled by the slider. In this instance, because the subject was a high-key scene, Lightroom automatically extended the Blacks slider range beyond its normal limit.

1 In this before version, the Basic panel settings were the default ones. The photograph lacks contrast, and this is confirmed by the Histogram panel.

2 In the Basic panel, I increased the Exposure setting slightly to obtain the desired lightness. I then adjusted the Whites slider so that the brightest points in this scene just started to clip and then eased off slightly. Meanwhile, I dragged the Blacks slider to the left to the point where the blacks just started to clip. Finally, I increased the Shadows amount to lighten the shadow detail on the boat.

3 The Basic panel adjustments made a dramatic improvement to the tone contrast, but I also wanted to bring out more subtle detail in the distance. Here, I placed a Graduated Filter adjustment where I added some Dehaze and reduced Vibrance.

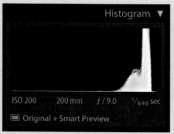

4 This shows the final, edited version where, as a result of the Graduated Filter adjustment, you can now see the hills in the distance more clearly. The overall feel of the image has remained true to the original scene. The highlight tones have been retained, but the increased contrast has resulted in the boat standing out more. The Histogram panel confirms that the image now has a fuller tone range and the delicate highlight detail has been preserved.

CLARITY ADJUSTMENTS

The Clarity slider is essentially a local-area contrast adjustment. The Clarity effect is achieved by adding variable amounts of contrast through a halo mask. In fact, the Highlights and Shadows sliders share the same underlying tone mask algorithm.

Adding positive amounts of Clarity can build up contrast in the midtone areas based on the edge detail in the photograph. Essentially, adding Clarity boosts the apparent contrast in the midtones but does so without affecting the overall global contrast. If, as you adjust an image, you try to squeeze in all the highlight and shadow detail, the tone separation can become flattened in the midtone areas. Therefore, where the detail in the midtone areas is compressed, you can add a little Clarity to enhance the midtone detail that lurks in the original capture image.

Many images will benefit from the addition of a small amount of Clarity. On the other hand, if you overdo it and add too much, the halos can become rather noticeable and your photographs will end up looking like badly processed HDR images. However, there are some types of photographs that will benefit from adding a large amount of Clarity. Over the next few pages you will see an example of how adding a maximum +100 Clarity helped expand the midtones in an image where the midtones were completely lacking contrast. With portrait photographs, high amounts of Clarity can be used to make the skin tones look extra gritty. Also, if you edit an HDR photo merge image, you can usually get away with adding a lot more Clarity than you would usually do when editing a regular raw capture image.

Clarity can be applied either as a global adjustment (via the Basic panel) or as a localized adjustment when using the Graduated Filter, Radial Filter, or Adjustment brush. Where there are particular areas that can benefit from the addition of Clarity, it is often best to apply this as a localized rather than a global adjustment.

Negative Clarity adjustments

A negative Clarity adjustment does the exact opposite of a positive Clarity adjustment. It can be used to soften the midtones and do so in a way that produces an effect not too dissimilar to traditional darkroom diffusion printing techniques. You can use this method to create some quite beautiful diffuse soft-focus image effects or to soften the skin tones in portrait photographs. I find negative Clarity adjustments work particularly well with black-and-white photographs, adding nice soft glows to the edge details.

Adding Clarity to bring out fine detail

This picture neatly sums up the misery and drama of a snowy day. As the photographer Andy Teasdale points out, "It shows the challenges and uncertainty of waiting for a public bus in rural Wales in the middle of winter." A scene like this is quite a challenge to photograph. Apart from the difficulty of taking photographs in freezing cold weather, there is the issue of how to expose correctly in snowy conditions. If the camera is set (as it was in this instance) to an automatic metering mode, the meter will have a tendency to underexpose in response to the whiteness of the scene. It is therefore a good idea to set the exposure compensation to +0.3 EV, or +0.6 EV, so that the camera's auto metering is biased toward giving you a brighter exposure setting. Better still, set the camera to manual mode, work out what the optimum ambient exposure setting should be, and keep it fixed to that setting.

It doesn't matter too much that the original photograph was a little underexposed because this was easily fixed in Lightroom. The important thing was to make sure the highlight detail was preserved as I lightened the image.

Photograph © Andy Teasdale

1 The overall scene looks rather dull and lacks contrast. Particular care was needed to bring out more detail in the bus stop shelter and, at the same time, preserve the highlight detail in the sky and snow.

2 To begin with, I clicked on the Auto button in the Basic panel (circled) to apply an Auto Tone adjustment. This instantly lightened the scene. I then selected the White Balance tool and clicked in the image (selecting the snow) to apply a calculated White Balance adjustment. This neutralized the blue cast that was in the original version.

3 I didn't want to lose any of the delicate highlight detail. I carefully adjusted the Basic panel settings to darken Highlights and at the same time I set the Clarity slider to a maximum +100 setting to boost the midtone contrast. I selected the Adjustment brush and used this to apply an Exposure lightening adjustment to the parent and child inside the bus shelter.

Photograph © Andy Teasdale

4 I then went to the Lens Corrections panel in Camera Raw and
applied an Auto Upright correction, combined with a -25 manual
Aspect slider adjustment (this
stretched the image horizontally).
Finally, I cropped the photograph
to remove the building that was
on the right.

TONE CURVE ADJUSTMENTS

While the Contrast slider in the Basic panel is just a single slider that can be used to increase or decrease the contrast, the Tone Curve panel (**Figure 3.7**) has four (parametric) Region sliders with which to fine-tune the contrast. These are Highlights, Lights, Darks, and Shadows, and as you adjust them they provide a shaded preview of the range of shapes the individual Tone Curve slider adjustments can make. These sliders can inspire you to create tone curves that are quite unlike any curve shape you might apply using the traditional point curve method.

The suggested workflow when tone adjusting an image is to do as much as you can in the Basic panel first. There are Photoshop purists who argue the Curves panel is the best tool with which to apply tone adjustments, and for pure Photoshop image editing this is true. But as has been shown earlier in this chapter, the depth of controls offered by the Basic panel in Lightroom and Camera Raw trumps what can be done with Curves adjustments alone. The Tone Curve panel in Lightroom is therefore an effective secondary tone editing tool to be applied after you have made all the Basic panel adjustments. It is therefore best to make the major tone contrast corrections using the Basic panel Contrast slider. If you do this, you will then have more headroom to make full use of the Lightroom Tone Curve panel controls to apply fine-tuned adjustments to the contrast. Splitting the contrast editing into two stages gives you increased range and control.

The tone range split points (just below the tone curve) allow you to restrict or broaden the range of tones that are affected by the four Tone Curve sliders. Adjusting each of the three tone range split points enables you to further fine-tune the shape of the curve. You can also manipulate the curve graph directly by clicking on a point on the curve and dragging up or down to modify that particular section of the curve, and you can use the up and down keyboard arrow keys to increase or decrease the tone values.

Point Curve mode

Lightroom can allow you to edit the tone curve the same way that you can using the Point Curve editor in Camera Raw (or the Curves adjustment in Photoshop). To switch to the Point Curve editing mode, click on the graph icon in the bottom right corner (circled red in Figure 3.7). Working in the Point Curve editing mode gives you the same degree of control as when working with the Curves panel in Photoshop—you can add as many curve points as you like and move them as you wish. To remove a point, you either need to use a right-click to open the contextual menu to delete a control point, double-click a point, or drag a point off the edge of the Tone Curve graph. Apart from the flexibility of the Point Curve editing mode, there is no difference between this and the parametric, slider mode of operation.

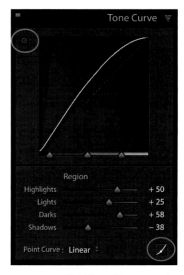

FIGURE 3.7 The Tone Curve panel.

NOTE

If you click to make the Target adjustment tool active (circled in blue in Figure 3.7), you can move the cursor over the image and click and drag upward to increase the lightness of the corresponding tone region slider, or drag downward to make the corresponding tone slider setting darker.

NOTE

The Snapshot panel is located in the left section of the Develop module, just below the Presets panel. If you click on the plus icon, you can save a current image state as a new snapshot.

BASIC PANEL AND TONE CURVE ADJUSTMENTS

When I edit a raw photograph, I usually aim to produce an optimized version using just the Basic panel adjustments, which can be regarded a baseline version to which further edits can be made. At this stage, it is often a good idea to save an optimized version as a baseline snapshot that you can easily revert to. Once I have done that, I can use the remaining tools in Lightroom, such as the Tone Curve and other Develop module panels, to add to the initial adjustment and produce different interpretations. Or, I may wish to re-edit the Basic panel settings as I create new versions. In the following steps, I show how the Basic panel settings were adjusted first to create an optimized version and how I afterward added a further contrast adjustment using the Tone Curve panel. The version I created at Step 3 was perfectly acceptable as an optimized image. What I did in Step 4 was to add a finishing touch with the addition of a Tone Curve panel adjustment.

1 Here is an image before I applied any adjustments. As you can see, the Histogram panel shows the tones are quite compressed.

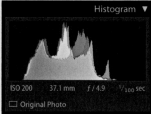

2 The first step was to lighten the image and boost the contrast, which I did by setting the Exposure to +0.30 and setting the Contrast to +34. At the same time, I fine-tuned the Whites and Blacks sliders and set the Shadows to +80 to bring out more detail in the darker areas of the picture.

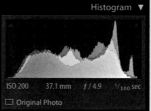

3 The midtones looked rather flat in Step 2, so I set the Clarity to +77 and increased Vibrance, setting it to +50. The Histogram panel now reveals how the levels are spread out nicely across the entire tone range. At this stage it would be a good idea to save these settings as a new snapshot.

4 In this final step, I went to Tone Curve and adjusted the Highlights, Lights, Darks and Shadows sliders to produce the tone curve shape shown here. I also adjusted the shadows tone range split point (circled), dragging this to the left so that the curve was steepened at the bottom end of the tone range. This refinement added a subtle kick to the shadow tones.

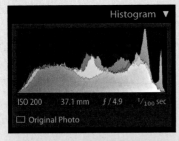

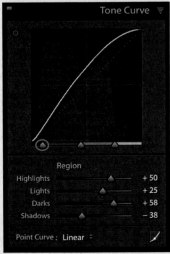

Tone range split point refinements

When you edit the tone curve, as you make the curve shape steeper this increases the contrast, and as you make the curve shape shallower it flattens the contrast. In the previous example, the tone curve was made steeper from the Shadows zone to the Lights but became shallower from the Lights to the Highlights zone. I also dragged the Shadows tone range split point fully to the left, and this caused the tone curve to rise more steeply from the darkest point. This meant the contrast increased sharply at the shadow end of the tone curve, with the contrast increase remaining continuous through the midtone-to-light areas. The contrast increase then began to drop off and became softer in the lightest areas. When I am editing a landscape photograph and I want to add more cloud contrast, I will sometimes add a Tone Curve adjustment and drag the Highlights slider to the right to lighten but also drag the Highlights tone range split point slider to the right as well. This can give a little kick to the highlights, adding more contrast to the clouds. With studio fashion or portrait photographs, I find it helps to apply a tone curve where contrast is added evenly to the shadows and the highlights, and I'll then push the Shadows and Highlights tone range split point sliders to their extremes. This applies a kick to the shadows and highlights, but with no midtone contrast boost, because this adjustment preserves a flat curve shape for the midtones (see **Figure 3.8**). You will find that by using the four Region sliders, you have plenty of control to manipulate the tone curve shape, and the three tone range split point sliders offer further fine-tuning control over the tone curve.

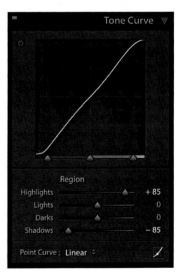

FIGURE 3.8 On the left is a tone-adjusted image, optimized using the Basic panel controls. On the right, a Tone Curve adjustment has been added in which the Shadows and Highlights tone range split point sliders were pushed to their extremes.

1 This shows how the raw file
looked when viewed in Lightroom
with no adjustments applied. I
liked the framing and there was
plenty of detail, but clearly something needed to be done to get
rid of the haze.

REDUCING HAZE

I shot this photograph recently from Ivinghoe Beacon, looking down on the road that
winds to the top of the hill, which is a particular favorite with cyclists. I like the way
the photograph was framed with the road forming an S shape. I also liked the road
markings, because this is indeed a steep hill to climb. It was shot with a 70–200 mm
zoom lens at the 200 mm setting using 1/400th second, f/3.5, and 200 ISO. Having
the camera mounted on a tripod helped keep the image nice and sharp, but because
the subject was quite far off, it was rather soft in contrast. This was down to the haze
rather than the lens optics. One way to tackle this is to use the Dehaze slider in the
Effects panel. By dragging to the right you can use Dehaze to remove haze, smoke,
or mist from a scene. As you do so, the adjustment can have quite a noticeable effect
on the saturation and enhance any edge vignetting that's present. You will therefore
find it is best to make sure you apply a lens profile correction (or a manual vignetting
correction) first to remove any lens vignetting and also set White Balance first before
you adjust the Dehaze slider.

2 In the Lightroom Develop module, I selected the White Balance tool and used this to click on the road to adjust the white balance and apply a custom setting for it.

3 I went to the Effects panel, where I adjusted the Dehaze slider, setting it to +40. This was enough to get rid of the haze and boost the contrast.

4 I then went to the Tone Curve panel and adjusted the sliders to give a kick to the highlight end of the tone curve. You will notice how I dragged the Highlights tone range slider to the right to fine-tune the contrast curve and focus on the extreme highlights tone range. In the Effects panel, I adjusted the Post-Crop Vignetting sliders to add a darkening vignette to the photograph. This helped concentrate attention more on the road and the cyclist.

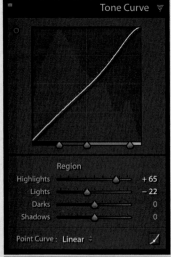

Localized haze reduction

Dehaze can also be applied as a localized adjustment. This makes the effect more useful for treating landscape images where, very often, the foreground at the bottom of the frame will look fine and it is only the subject matter in the distance from the middle to the top of the frame that needs correcting. A Dehaze effect can have a very destructive effect if applied to the areas that don't need it, so it is great that you can apply such corrections using the localized adjustment tools.

1 This landscape photograph was also shot using a long focus lens, where I applied the Basic panel adjustments shown here to optimize the tone contrast.

2 I then selected the Graduated Filter tool and applied the adjustment settings shown here to the top half of the photograph in order to darken it slightly and bring out more detail in the distant hills and clouds. Notice how I also needed to reduce Vibrance to counter the saturation boost that resulted from the +40 Dehaze adjustment.

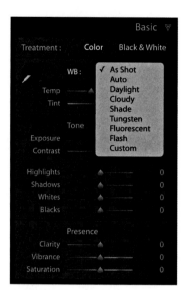

FIGURE 3.9 The Basic panel showing the White Balance menu options.

COLOR ADJUSTMENTS

Color adjustments should begin as soon as you bring your images into Lightroom. In the last chapter, we looked at setting the camera profile via the Camera Calibration panel, the effect this can have on color rendering, and why it is a good idea to establish this as a per-camera default Develop setting. Now let's look at the other color adjustments in more detail.

WHITE BALANCING

At the top of the Basic panel is the White Balance section. Here, you can select a preset from the White Balance menu (**Figure 3.9**), drag the Temp and Tint sliders to apply a custom white balance, or choose the White Balance Selector tool to undock it from the panel and manually select a target color in the image to set the desired white balance (see "Applying a Custom White Balance Adjustment"). Once you have set the white balance in this way, all the colors should look correct.

The main thing to bear in mind here is that when setting the white balance, you are not adjusting the white balance of the actual scene, you are "assigning" a setting to a photograph that's already been shot. Therefore, if you drag the Temp slider to the right and assign a higher Temp value, you are telling Lightroom the white balance recorded by the camera was too low, which resulted in the photo appearing too blue. A higher Temp value will make the image warmer and therefore more neutral in color. Think of it this way—if you were to shoot with a tungsten-balanced film in daylight conditions, the result would be a blue image. You would need to add a warming filter in front of the lens to get the tungsten-balanced film to record daylight scenes that look neutral in color. The Tint slider adds a further dimension to a White Balance adjustment, allowing you to compensate for green/magenta tints that can occur, for example, when shooting under fluorescent lighting conditions.

If you use the White Balance Selector tool to set white balance, it is important to click on an area of the image that is actually neutral in color. This should be something that is white or light gray but not pure white. If one or more of the color channels is clipped in this area, this will give a false reading. As you can see in the following example, I selected an area of the driver's helmet that was slightly shaded and off-white in color.

VIBRANCE AND SATURATION

At the bottom of the Basic panel are the Vibrance and Saturation sliders. These can both be used to increase or decrease the saturation. Of the two, the Vibrance slider is the most useful because it has a clipping prevention mechanism that stops colors that are already saturated from becoming clipped. So, as you increase the vibrance

APPLYING A CUSTOM WHITE BALANCE ADJUSTMENT

1 This shows a photograph taken at Goodwood Revival using the auto White Balance setting on the camera, where the Basic panel shows the As Shot setting.

2 In the Basic panel I selected the White Balance tool to undock it from the panel and then clicked in the image to select a target neutral color. In undocked mode the rectangular loupe overlay can help guide you in your image selection. In this instance, I clicked on the shaded area of the white helmet of one of the drivers to set the white balance.

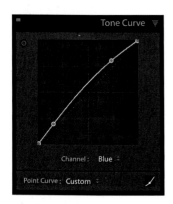

FIGURE 3.10 An example of a fashion image processed using negative Vibrance.

the slider applies a saturation increase to all colors except those that are already fully saturated. You can use the Saturation slider if you prefer, but if you wish to avoid any clipping it is nearly always better to use Vibrance instead. Dragging in the other direction allows you to reduce the saturation. A -100 Vibrance setting will produce a muted color effect, whereas a -100 Saturation adjustment will produce a monochrome result.

It can be tempting to add Vibrance to all your color photographs, but I do recommend you explore the subtle, pastel colors you get when you apply negative Vibrance. For example, the fashion photograph in **Figure 3.10** was processed in Lightroom using a -70 Vibrance setting to achieve a muted color effect.

RGB CURVES

Earlier in this chapter I mentioned how you can switch to the point curve editing mode, by clicking on the icon in the bottom-right corner of the Tone Curve panel. This mode also gives you the option to independently edit the Red, Green, and Blue channel curves, just as you can in Photoshop when using a Curves adjustment. Although you can apply Photoshop principles to Tone Curve panel RGB adjustments, I advise you to use the White Balance tools in the Basic panel to set the white balance and use the Contrast and Vibrance sliders to achieve the desired contrast and saturation. The Tone Curve panel can be used to apply RGB curves adjustments that either enhance the colors further or apply different types of color effects (see **Figure 3.11**).

FIGURE 3.11 On the left is an image with the default settings applied and on the right, a version where I applied a Tone Curve RGB point curve adjustment.

BOOSTING THE COLOR SATURATION

1 There were a lot of colorful elements in the original raw capture. The exposure was spot-on, but more needed to be done in postprocessing to enhance the color.

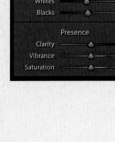

2 A few initial Basic panel edits were applied in this step. This included setting the Highlights slider to -100 and the Shadows slider to +100 to enhance the detail in the highlights and the shadows.

3 In this step, a +20 Clarity adjustment added more midtone contrast and a +85 Vibrance adjustment boosted the color, but without letting the already saturated colors clip.

4 A Radial Filter adjustment was then added, set to Outside mode. The Exposure slider was set to -0.30 to darken the area outside the Radial Filter selection. The Tint slider was set to -28 to apply a slight green tint to emphasize the foliage colors.

5 Here is the final version, where the Clone Stamp tool and Healing brush were used to fill in the top-right and bottom-right corners. This picture, a photograph of Sue Kreitzman, was photographed by Ansell Cizic for his series of portraits of artisans and artists of the East End. Kreitzman, a native New Yorker and former food writer, now lives and works as an artist in London.

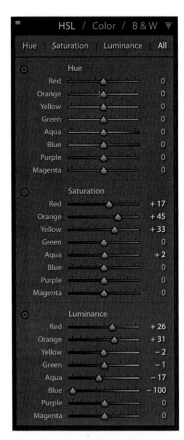

FIGURE 3.12 The HSL/Color/B&W panel in HSL All mode.

FIGURE 3.13 The HSL/Color/B&W panel in HSL Luminance mode.

HSL/COLOR/B&W PANEL

The HSL/Color/B&W panel (**Figure 3.12**) can be used in HSL mode to apply color-selective hue, saturation, or luminance adjustments to color images. The Color mode allows you to do just the same, except with a slightly different interface, while the B&W mode can be used to convert a color image to black and white and adjust the tone brightness of the color components that make up a black-and-white conversion. Figure 3.12 shows the HSL panel controls in All mode where the Hue, Saturation, and Luminance slider controls are all accessible at once. **Figure 3.13** shows the HSL controls with the Luminance mode selected.

You will notice that the eight color slider controls include Orange, Aqua, and Purple sliders. The reasoning behind this is that the slider colors listed here more typically reflect the color ranges most photographers are actually interested in editing, as opposed to the usual list of Red, Green, Blue, Cyan, Magenta, and Yellow controls you will find in the Photoshop Hue/Saturation image adjustment dialog.

The Hue sliders can be used to modify the hue values for the Red, Orange, and Yellow colors and others. There aren't too many applications for this type of adjustment unless you wish to deliberately change the hue for specific colors in an image or there is a problem with the spectral response of the camera sensor. For example, the sensors in older digital cameras had the tendency to give Caucasian skin tones a California suntan look. Such images can be improved by selecting the Orange Hue slider and dragging it to the right to make orange colors a little more yellow.

The Saturation sliders let you modify the saturation of the target colors, thereby allowing you to selectively boost or lower the saturation for specific colors.

In my view, the Luminance sliders are the most useful of all because they can be used to modify the luminance of the selected target colors to make them appear lighter or darker. The following step-by-step example shows the dramatic effect HSL Luminance slider adjustments can have on an image. When you click on the little button icon in the top-left corner to activate the Target Adjustment tool (see Step 3), you can move the tool cursor over the image and modify the values for the target colors below where you click and drag. Dragging upward increases the setting value, while dragging downward decreases it. When you do this, Lightroom selects a principal and secondary color slider and adjusts both as you drag. In the following tutorial, you will see I targeted the blue sky and dragged the cursor downward: this adjusted mainly the Blue but also the Aqua slider. In this particular example, the effect is similar to placing an adjustable polarizing filter over the lens. However, adjusting the image digitally is not the same as doing it in-camera, and you may sometimes see halos appearing around the edges where there are contrasting colors. It can look worse onscreen than it will in print, but, still, this highlights the deficiencies of trying to do too much at the postproduction stage.

Modifying the color using HSL adjustments

1 Here is a raw image before any Develop settings had been applied.

2 In this step, I set White Balance to the Daylight setting and adjusted the Tone sliders to optimize the image. I also boosted the Clarity and Vibrance settings.

3 I then went to the HSL/Color/B&W panel, where I selected the Luminance tab and Target Adjustment Tool (circled) and dragged downward on the sky area to selectively darken the target colors: in this case the Aqua and Blue sliders.

4 I kept the Target Adjustment tool active and clicked on the houseboats to modify the luminance values there, making Red and Orange lighter. Finally, I selected the Saturation tab and dragged on the image to selectively boost the color saturation for Red, Orange, and Yellow.

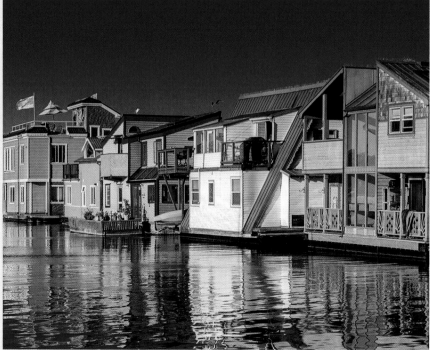

4

DODGING AND BURNING

AND WHY WHAT YOU SEE IS NOT ALWAYS WHAT YOU GET

WHY WE NEED TO MANIPULATE OUR IMAGES

There is nothing new about image manipulation. Photographers have been doing this in the darkroom long before technology gave us the tools to process our photographs digitally. If you study the work of well-known photographers, such as Sebastião Salgado and Josef Koudelka, you will discover just how much dodging and burning was done at the darkroom stage to create some of their most iconic images. Some photographers still regard this as cheating. Perhaps they assume the camera faithfully records everything they saw at the time the picture was taken. However, if you consider how our eyes actually perceive the world, you'll realize this isn't the case. Our eyes constantly adapt as we look at the things around us, and what we think we perceive as reality isn't. This is because of the brain's ability to interpret what our eyes see and build a picture in our mind where everything appears to be correctly lit. There are limits, of course. We all know how difficult it is to see in the dark and how you would be ill-advised to go looking for sunspots through a telescope. But in everyday situations, our brain does this amazing conjuring trick where it cons us into believing the lighting in a scene is evenly balanced, when in fact it might well not be. For instance, when you look at a large white wall, your brain will perceive this to be evenly white, whereas if you were to take a photograph of the wall the image you capture will reveal the slightest variations in illumination. This is why for studio photography it is important to use a light meter to help determine the evenness of your lighting, rather than rely on what you think you see with your eyes.

When you photograph outdoors, there can be as much as several stops between the exposure required to capture the sky and that needed to record the foreground. Again, our brain doesn't notice this—it compiles an idealized version of the scene in front of us, one the camera can't always hope to match unless you are able to compensate for this at the capture stage or in postprocessing. Landscape photographers typically place a neutral density graduated filter over the front of the lens to darken the sky relative to the land. That's one way you can approach the problem. Another is to use the Graduated Filter tool in Lightroom to add a darkening effect, like the example in **Figure 4.1**.

FIGURE 4.1 The top image shows a landscape photograph of Bryce Canyon, which I processed in Lightroom, where I adjusted the tones to produce the best optimized version for the foreground. The lower version shows the same image, where a Graduated Filter adjustment was added to darken the clouds. This version is probably closer in appearance to how the scene was perceived at the time.

HOW YOUR CAMERA SEES

A digital camera records light values in a linear fashion, where the signal output of the sensor doubles for every EV stop increase in exposure. That is to say, as you open the lens aperture one stop, or double the exposure time, you increase the exposure by one stop and the sensor signal output is doubled. Typically, a sensor may be capable of capturing up to 4,000 levels of tone. When an image is captured and digitally converted (and gamma-corrected), around 2,000 levels will be used to describe the brightest stop value, 1,000 levels to record the next stop down in exposure, 500 the next, and so on. At the same time you have to bear in mind the optimum exposure setting is the point at which you can expose an image without clipping the highlights. As the light levels arriving at the sensor are increased, you reach the point where the photosites on the sensor become saturated with photons and are therefore unable to record additional photons. This determines the sensor's white clipping point.

The raw image recorded by the sensor will also look rather dark compared with the way we interpret light hitting our retinas. In order to make a digital capture look like a recognizable image, a gamma-correcting curve has to be applied to the raw data. This is essentially a midpoint lightening adjustment, which effectively stretches the shadow levels further apart and compresses the highlight levels closer together. Therefore, a correctly exposed digital capture image (whether it is converted by the camera processor to produce a JPEG or is a raw file converted in Lightroom) will appear similar to how we viewed a scene, but not quite the same, because of the difference in the way our brain compensates for varying levels of illumination in different areas of the scene. And, as a result of the gamma correction, most of the levels information will be compressed in the highlights, while fewer levels will be available to edit the shadow areas.

LOCALIZED ADJUSTMENTS

The Lightroom Develop module has three types of localized adjustment tools: Graduated Filter, Radial Filter, and the Adjustment brush. The localized adjustment sliders in Figure 4.1 are the same for each of these tools. They provide a wide range of options and are more or less direct equivalents of those found in the Basic panel. The exceptions are the Saturation slider, which is a hybrid of Vibrance and Saturation, and the Sharpness slider, which is effectively a Detail panel sharpening Amount slider, and similarly, the Noise slider, which is a Detail panel noise reduction Luminance slider. For darkening and lightening you can use the Exposure slider, but you can also use the localized adjustment tools to apply Tint adjustments, add more Clarity, or decrease Saturation. The possibilities are endless, although there are some particular combinations I find are good to use; I'll show you these later in this chapter. Let's dive in and look at how I was able to combine the use of the Radial Filter with the Graduated Filter to build up a series of localized edits to reshape the lighting in the following image example.

Basic dodging and burning

Basic

Treatment : Color | Black & White

WB : As Shot

Temp — 5,300
Tint — + 12

Tone | Auto
Exposure — 0.00
Contrast — 0

Highlights — 0
Shadows — 0
Whites — 0
Blacks — 0

Presence
Clarity — 0
Vibrance — 0
Saturation — 0

1 This is a photograph I took of my cousin, Marek, while visiting his studio, Marek Music, in Canada. I photographed him at work using just the available daylight.

Basic

Treatment : Color | Black & White

WB : Custom

Temp — 10,619
Tint — + 12

Tone | Auto
Exposure — − 0.30
Contrast — 0

Highlights — − 11
Shadows — + 73
Whites — 0
Blacks — 0

Presence
Clarity — + 23
Vibrance — 0
Saturation — 0

2 I wanted the room to look darker and make it appear to be lit with tungsten lighting. To do this, I dragged the Temp slider to the right to set a warmer white balance and decreased the Exposure.

3 I then selected the Radial Filter tool, clicked on Marek's chest, and dragged outward. The Exposure slider was set to -1.38, which applied a feathered, darkening exposure adjustment to the area outside the Radial Filter ellipse.

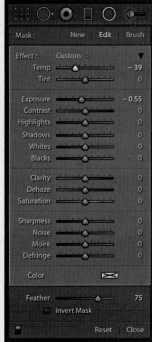

4 With the Radial Filter still active, I clicked on the New button to add a second Radial Filter adjustment. Again, I clicked on Marek's chest, but this time defined a smaller ellipse. I dragged the Temp slider to the left so that the outside area would have a less warm color cast and set the Exposure to -0.55 to add some extra darkening.

5 Next, I selected the Graduated Filter adjustment, dragged from the right side of the image inward to the center, and set the Exposure amount to +1.95. This adjustment effectively canceled out the two Radial Filter adjustments for this portion of the image. Therefore, I was using the Graduated Filter here as an undo adjustment to restore the original luminance to this portion of the photograph.

6 I liked how the image looked in color, but I also created the black-and-white version you can see here.

Refining filter adjustments

In the previous step-by-step, the Radial Filter adjustments were applied using the default settings for the Feather and mask. This meant that the filter adjustments were applied to the areas outside the Radial Filter area and the Feather amount was 75. You can fine-tune the Feather setting to create a harder or softer feather edge when applying Radial Filter adjustments. Clicking the Invert mask option applies the adjustment to inside the Radial Filter area, which is useful if you want to select a specific area to apply the adjustment to. Typically, you might want to use the Radial Filter in this way to add cumulative adjustments, such as a series of lightening or darkening effects, where applying these as multiple filters allows you to define an area more precisely. To edit a filter adjustment, make sure the filter is active and the edit pins are made visible. If you know you have applied a filter adjustment but can't see the pins, check the Show Edit Pins menu in the Toolbar, or press the Ⓗ key to make them visible again. To move a filter adjustment, click the radio button in the middle and drag.

When working with the Graduated Filter tool, you can adjust the angle and width of a Graduated Filter effect by dragging on the overlay directly. To rotate, move the cursor along the central overlay line till you see a double-headed arrow cursor and click and drag. To adjust the width, click on either of the outer lines and click and drag to make the filter edge harder or softer. With Radial Filter adjustments, move the cursor outside the radius overlay and click and drag to rotate. Click and drag the handles directly to edit the shape of the Radial Filter overlay (see **Figure 4.2**).

FIGURE 4.2 The Filter overlay controls that are available when working with the Graduated and Radial Filters.

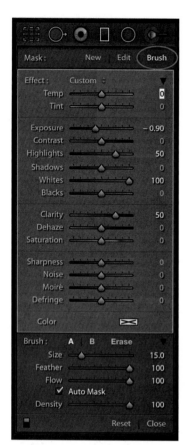

FIGURE 4.3 The Graduated Filter options in Brush edit mode with the brush options at the bottom. Brush A is currently selected.

TIP

You can hold down the [Alt] key when painting in Brush mode to temporarily switch to the Erase mode and vice versa.

Editing skies with the Graduated Filter

Figure 4.1 showed how to darken a sky by adding a negative Exposure Graduated Filter adjustment. This can work well in a lot of situations and is similar to placing a neutral density filter over the lens at the time of shooting. But there are other sliders to play with that can do more than just darken. You can use the Temp slider to make a sky appear warmer or cooler and use the Contrast slider to add more contrast. Subtle effects can be achieved using different combinations of Exposure, Highlights, Whites, and Clarity adjustments. For example, the Highlights slider can be used to make the cloud highlight detail darker or lighter. It all depends on the image and the brightness of the clouds in the scene, but a move either way can make the clouds stand out more. With the Whites slider, I find a positive Whites adjustment can be effective if you need to add more contrast to the highlight areas, especially if you mix an Exposure darkening with a positive Whites adjustment. The Clarity slider can be very helpful for adding more contrast to the midtone areas. With dark, cloudy skies that have lots of interesting cloud detail, you can increase Clarity to add more definition. I suggest you experiment with all these sliders to see which ones will help make the clouds stand out best. You can sometimes even add a Shadows adjustment into the mix.

Brush editing the mask

If you click the Brush button (circled in **Figure 4.3**), this switches you to the Brush edit mode, where it is possible to edit the mask for a Graduated or Radial Filter adjustment. Here, you have the option to configure separate Brush A and Brush B settings and paint on the image to define the areas you wish to add the filter effect to. Or, you can switch to the Erase mode to define the areas where you wish to remove the filter effect. The Size slider refers to the size of the brush, while the Feather slider determines how hard or soft the brush will be. The Flow slider can be used to control the rate at which the brushwork is applied. For instance, you can drag this to a low Flow setting and use multiple brushstrokes to build the brush opacity. The Density slider determines the maximum density that can be achieved when using a brush to edit the mask. If you are using a Wacom or similar tablet device, you can set Flow and Density to 100 and use pen pressure to determine the flow rate and density.

When the Auto Mask option is checked, where you first click records a sample color selection and uses this to limit the extent of the brushwork. In other words, if you click on, say, an area of blue sky, this creates something like a hidden magic wand selection of the blue sky area that constrains the extent of your brushwork. As you release the mouse and click again, this creates a new selection. It should be pointed out that the edges created as a result of using the Auto Mask mode can sometimes appear a little ragged. It is therefore best to carry out such brushwork at a 1:1 view so you can monitor it carefully.

Brush editing a Graduated Filter adjustment

1 This photograph of Stonehenge was captured in the late afternoon, with a lovely cloudy sky. This shows what the image looked like with the default Develop settings applied.

2 In the Basic panel, I adjusted the tone sliders to darken the Highlights slightly and adjusted the Whites and Blacks sliders to expand the tone range and add more contrast. I also set Clarity to +20 to add more midtone contrast.

3 I then selected the Graduated Filter tool and dragged from just above the horizon downward to barely below the base of the stones. I set the Exposure to -0.90 to darken the clouds. At the same time, I increased the Highlights and Whites settings to add more highlight contrast. I also raised Clarity to add midtone contrast.

4 Having done that, I clicked to switch to Brush edit mode for the Graduated Filter and with Show Selected Mask Overlay checked in the Toolbar, used the Erase brush mode with Auto Mask enabled to remove the stones from the Graduated Filter mask.

5 This shows the final version, where, if you compare with Step 3, you can see how masking the stones using the Brush edit Erase mode for the Graduated Filter tool allowed the filter adjustment to be applied to the graduated areas only, except for the mask-defined outline of the stones. If you compare the stone lintels in this version and the previous one, you will notice there is no darkening in these areas. It is worth mentioning here that when you brush-edit a Graduated or Radial Filter adjustment, the Brush edit mask remains independent of the filter adjustment. Therefore, with this image I could revisit the Graduated Filter and edit the range of the Graduated Filter adjustment independent of the Brush edit defined mask outline. The only other thing I did here was to go to the HSL/Color/B&W panel, where I lightened the grass and darkened the stones slightly.

FIGURE 4.4 The Adjustment brush controls.

Adjustment brush settings

The Adjustment brush controls (**Figure 4.4**) are the same as those for the Graduated and Radial Filters, but with the addition of the brush controls at the bottom. These are identical to the brush controls for the Graduated and Radial Filter brush modes that I described earlier.

Basically, the Adjustment brush allows you to apply freeform brush edits, which can be defined by applying single or multiple brushstrokes. Where you first click with the Adjustment brush will add a pin overlay to the image, and as you carry on brushing you will add to the defined area linked to that pin marker. You can use the Size, Feather, and Flow sliders to control the brush cursor and brush behavior and use the Erase mode to erase your brushwork. If you have a Wacom tablet and stylus, you can use varying amounts of stylus pressure to control the opacity, which can give you a fine degree of control over your painting. Once you have added a brushstroke, you can adjust the sliders to achieve the desired adjustment setting. If you want to add a new set of brushstrokes with a different combination of settings, you will need to click the New button at the top to exit the current pin editing and click again to apply a new Adjustment brush pin. A quick tip here is to press the q or r key when applying a brush adjustment to exit from the Edit mode and switch to the New mode, so that when you next click on the preview you will add a new pin.

Each time you add a new pin, this effectively adds a mask that records the brush edit information. This does increase the file size of the metadata, but not by as much as you would think, because the mask data is compressed. A bigger problem is what happens when you add multiple Adjustment brush pins. The Lightroom processing required to render a preview is quite intense. This is because Lightroom has to calculate the main slider adjustments, plus, in addition, the mask-defined brush adjustments. Every time you add a brush adjustment, Lightroom has to continually update the Develop preview on the fly. As you add extra Adjustment brush pins, you are adding to the complexity and effectively multiplying the problem. It is therefore best to keep the number of pins to as few as possible. Once you add up to five pins or more, you may see a significant slowdown in the Lightroom Develop module performance. Elsewhere in the program, Lightroom does not have a problem managing images that contain complex brush edits. This is because the other Lightroom modules all reference cached preview files instead.

Combining multiple localized adjustments

The location in this photograph, which was shot by Chris Evans, is a fairly ordinary service corridor that was livened up by placing a direct flash head to the right and slightly above the head height of the subject and synchronizing this with a second head, placed farther down the corridor and facing directly toward the camera with a strong blue gel on it. This provided the strong backlighting and added a blue color to the background. The flash lighting was also balanced with the corridor lighting, allowing the ambient exposure to be bright enough to record these other lights. As you can imagine, a lot of steps were required to achieve the end result. Most of this was done through the use of dodging and burning to produce a more dramatic lighting effect.

In this tutorial, you will notice how a Clarity adjustment can be applied as an Adjustment brush setting to enhance the skin tone contrast in a portrait photograph. This technique first emerged when photographers began experimenting with Photomatix Pro to process single-exposure portrait images. They noticed how, by adding more midtone detail contrast, they could achieve gritty, textured portraits. The Clarity slider in Camera Raw and Lightroom can also be used to achieve this kind of look by applying the effect as a localized adjustment.

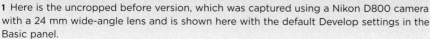

1 Here is the uncropped before version, which was captured using a Nikon D800 camera with a 24 mm wide-angle lens and is shown here with the default Develop settings in the Basic panel.

2 The first step was to go to the Lens Corrections panel and apply a Vertical Upright correction. I then selected the Crop Overlay tool, cropped to remove the fluorescent light that was directly above the man's head, and tightened the crop to remove the corridor corner that was visible on the left.

3 Next, I selected the Radial Filter tool and applied three lightening adjustments. I also added a Temp adjustment to the jacket to make it more blue and a Tint adjustment to the face to make it less magenta.

4 I then selected the Graduated Filter tool and applied the three adjustments shown here. One was used to darken the top, another to darken the left, and another to darken the right, using a -1.35 Exposure adjustment.

5 In this step, I selected the Adjustment brush, where I applied a darkening adjustment to the ceiling and a darkening adjustment to the corridor, with a blue Temp setting, and made a third adjustment to the face and body, where I applied a +100 Clarity adjustment.

Photograph: © Chris Evans

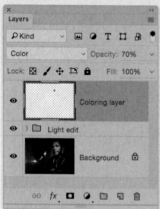

6 Finally, I opened the raw image as a TIFF in Photoshop, where I added a few further edits. The light in the background had clipped highlights that resulted in some sharp banding. To correct this, I added a combination of local noise, blur, and localized Hue/ Saturation to smooth out the edges. There was also a blue clip light hitting just above the bridge of the nose. To remove this, I added a new layer set to Color mode and sampled local colors and painted with the Brush tool.

ADDING AN EFFECTS PANEL VIGNETTE

The Post-Crop Vignetting options in the Effects panel (**Figure 4.5**) provide a really simple way to burn in the corners of the frame, according to how the image is cropped. On the face of it, adding a post-crop vignette will appear to undo a lens profile correction adjustment. The thing is, with some photographs the inherent lens vignetting is a distraction, and photographers will want their pictures to appear evenly exposed from the center to the corners of the frame, which is why it is a good thing to apply a lens profile correction. But sometimes it is more aesthetically pleasing for the vignetting to be left in. This is because the inclusion or addition of a vignette can help direct the eye to the center of the picture. I prefer to have the Enable Profile Corrections option checked in the Lens Corrections panel so that a geometric and vignetting correction is always applied and then choose to add post-crop vignetting effects where I feel it is necessary or useful to do so. It may not always be apparent that a post-crop vignette is required. What I find happens is that as you edit the tones in a photo to produce a version where the shadows in the main subject are filled in more, these tonal adjustments can leave the surrounding areas looking rather flat. Adding a darkening post-crop vignette can therefore add more depth to such images. If I think the tone editing is at the stage where a post-crop vignette will benefit the image, I will do so at the end. **Figure 4.6** shows an example of where Post-Crop Vignetting was added to a photograph.

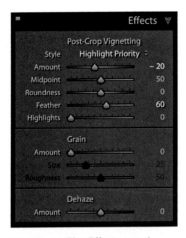

FIGURE 4.5 The Effects panel showing the Post-Crop Vignetting options.

FIGURE 4.6 On the left is an image with no post-crop vignette and on the right, the same photo using the Post-Crop Vignetting settings shown in the Effects panel.

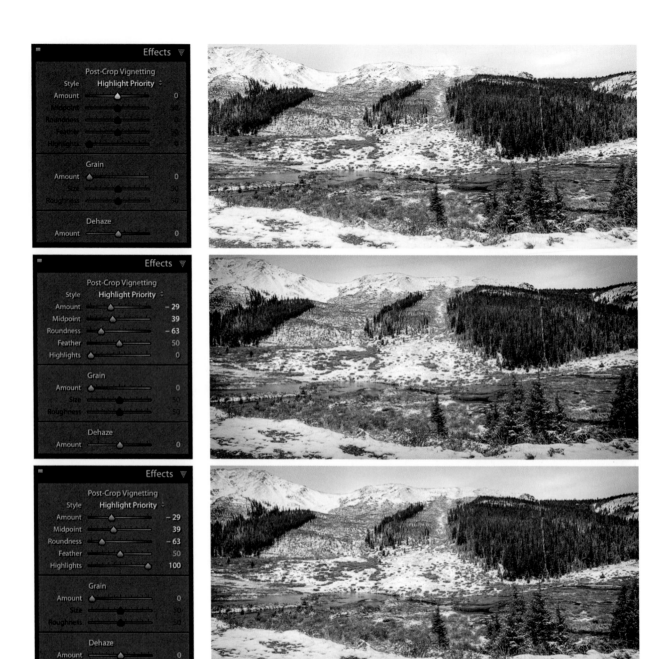

FIGURE 4.7 An example of a Highlight Priority post-crop vignette effect with and without a Highlights slider adjustment.

Post-Crop Vignetting options

In the Style menu you are best off ignoring the Paint Overlay option and choosing either the Highlight Priority or Color Priority options. Highlight Priority produces a more pronounced effect as it applies the post-crop vignette prior to the Exposure adjustment and provides better highlight recovery at the expense of producing unwanted color shifts in the highlight areas.

The wintry panorama in **Figure 4.7** was shot just outside Aspen, Colorado. The top image shows the before version without any Effects panel settings, while the middle image has a Highlight Priority post-crop vignette applied to it. With the bottom image, the Highlights slider was set to +100. If you look carefully at the edges, you will notice how this preserved more of the highlight detail. The image still has a vignette applied to it, but the effect is now less obvious in the highlights, and the edge darkening has become more concentrated in the shadow regions.

The Color Priority option produces a more gentle post-crop effect, which is applied after the Basic panel Exposure adjustment but before Tone Curve adjustments. This helps minimize color shifts in the darkened areas but won't apply any highlight recovery. I recommend you try the Highlight Priority option first, and if that looks too strong, choose the Color Priority method instead. With either of these methods, whenever you apply a negative setting, the Highlights slider will be active. This can be used to increase the contrast in the midtone to highlight tone areas (but not in the darker midtones). Basically, increasing Highlights counteracts the Post-Crop Vignetting effect in the brighter areas, such as the sky, but has less effect where the vignetting affects the darker areas of an image.

PHOTOSHOP ADJUSTMENTS

Lightroom localized adjustments are great because they are, in most instances, quick and easy to apply. That is, until you attempt to apply complex edits using the Adjustment brush. It is possible to use the Adjustment brush to do all sorts of things, like hand color a photograph, but as I pointed out earlier, if you make a complex selection or start adding multiple pins, Lightroom's performance soon slows down. The same is also true if you extensively use the Spot Removal tool in Lightroom. Where the benefits of using Lightroom become outweighed by the processing overhead, it is time to switch to Photoshop to carry out complex image-editing tasks. This is because Photoshop is quicker for brush painting and retouching work and makes for a more versatile and flexible workflow. It therefore helps to have a good understanding of Photoshop image adjustments and how to apply localized adjustments nondestructively.

1 Here, you can see a photograph I edited in raw mode with the default Basic panel settings.

2 I optimized the image in Lightroom to achieve the desired contrast and then opened it in Photoshop, where I applied the Clone stamp and Spot healing brush tools to retouch the photo.

3 I used the Lasso tool to make a selection of the eyes. I then clicked on the Adjustment menu (circled in the Layers panel) and selected Curves. This added a Curves adjustment layer and automatically added a layer mask based on the Lasso selection. Here, I added the curve points shown below in the Properties panel to add more contrast and gently lighten the whites of the eyes (but not so much that it would make the eyes look as if they had been artificially lightened). I also placed this adjustment layer in a new layer group titled "Hair and eyes."

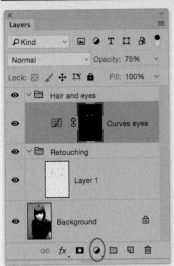

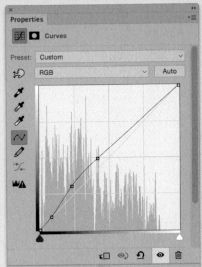

4 I added a second Curves adjustment layer and used the [Alt] [Del] keys to fill the Curves layer mask with black (where black was the default foreground color in the Tools panel). A black mask will hide any adjustment and white will reveal it. Making white now the foreground color and with the mask still active, I selected the Brush tool and painted over the hair. I went to the Properties panel and added a Curve point to lighten the curve and add more contrast to the shadows. I then reselected the Brush tool and fine-tuned the mask. I made the mask visible here by selecting it in the Channels panel.

5 This shows the final image where the Curves adjustment selectively added lightness and contrast to the hair. As the Curves adjustment blend mode was set to Normal, this contrast boost increased the saturation as well.

Client: Russell Eaton. Model: Christine Lecoeur @ M&P Models

FIGURE 4.8 The Layers panel showing the adjustment layer options.

TIP

You can also use the Dodge and Burn tools in Photoshop to lighten or darken an overlay-neutral gray layer.

Adding masked adjustment layers

The previous example showed how it is possible to add a Curves adjustment as an adjustment layer. To do this, go to the Layers panel, mouse down on the Adjustment layer menu, and select the adjustment you want to apply (see **Figure 4.8**). This adds an adjustment layer above the current selected layer, which is applied globally to all the layers below the adjustment layer. I typically select Curves to apply lightening or darkening adjustments, but you can choose any of the items listed in Figure 4.8 to apply other types of adjustments as well. When you add a new adjustment layer, the adjustment layer mask will be filled with white. This applies the adjustment to the entire canvas. If you set Black as the foreground color in the Tools panel and use ad to fill the mask with black, this hides the adjustment completely. If you then select the Brush tool and paint with white (or add a white to black gradient), you can selectively unhide the adjustment and apply it to the selected areas (as was shown in the previous step-by-step).

If you a-click the gap between an adjustment layer and the layer below, this clips the adjustment layer to the contents of that layer. That is to say, if the layer contains an image element or a graphic shape, when you apply a clipped adjustment, the effect is applied to the contents of that layer and no others.

ADDING OVERLAY LAYERS

Another way you can add a localized adjustment in Photoshop is to add a neutral adjustment layer and change the layer blend mode. If you a-click the Create a new layer button, this pops up the New Layer dialog, which allows you to select the layer blend mode for the new layer. Below that is a Fill with Overlay-neutral color option, which is available for all the layer blend modes, except Dissolve, Hard Mix, Hue, Saturation, Color, and Luminosity. This allows you to create a new layer filled with an overlay-neutral color. For example, with the Screen mode, Black is the neutral color and with Multiply, it is white. For the Overlay, Soft Light, and Hard Light modes, the neutral color is 50% gray. If you add a new layer filled with a neutral color, it will have no effect on the layers below until you modify the layer color. So, if you select the Screen blend mode and paint with white, this applies a lightening adjustment, which you can undo by painting with black again, or you can achieve in-between results by painting with varying shades of gray.

The Overlay, Soft Light, and Hard Light modes are interesting, as these increase contrast. Here, the overlay-neutral color is 50% gray. Painting with a light gray or white has more of an effect lightening the light colors and less so on the darker tones, while painting with dark gray or black has more of an effect on the darker tones. The Overlay blend mode effect is quite strong, the Hard Light mode even stronger, but Soft Light applies a nice, delicate contrast adjustment. For some specific tasks, it is a good technique to be aware of. Most of the time I find adding a Curves adjustment layer and editing the layer mask is better because you have fine control of the tone adjustments and masking.

Using overlay layers to apply local adjustments

The following steps show how I was able to add an overlay-neutral layer and adjust the layer blend mode to produce different types of localized adjustment effects.

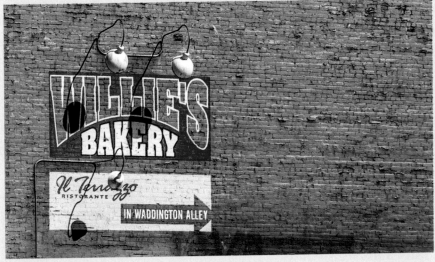

1 This photograph was optimized in Lightroom and opened in Photoshop. In this step I ⎡Alt⎤-clicked the Add new layer button in the Layers panel (circled).

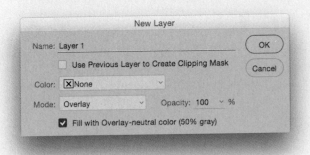

2 This opened the New Layer dialog. From the Mode menu, I selected the Overlay layer blend mode, which in turn allowed me to check the Fill with overlay-neutral color (50% gray) option. When I clicked OK, this added a new layer with the layer blend mode set to Overlay filled with a 50% neutral gray color. The neutral gray had no effect on the image below.

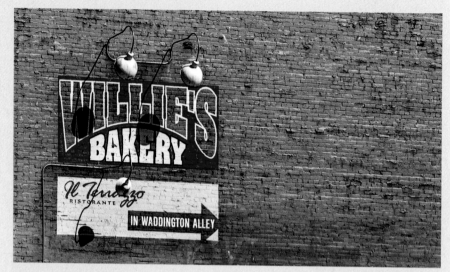

3 I was now able to modify the overlay-neutral layer to make it darker or lighter than a 50% midgray. In this instance, I selected the Brush tool, and with a slightly darker gray selected as the foreground color, painted on the layer to add more density plus more contrast to the selected areas. I also selected a lighter gray color to paint the bottom area to lighten (see the modified layer thumbnail).

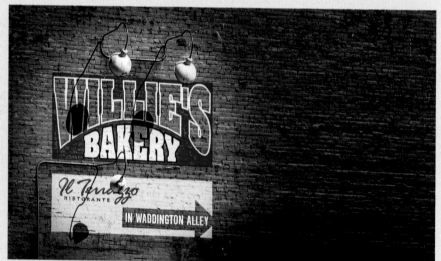

4 This shows an alternative version, where I reverted to Step 2 and changed the layer blend mode to Multiply. In this example, the 50% gray applied an overall darkening adjustment to the image. I selected white as the foreground color and painted on the layer to remove the Multiply effect (because white has no effect in Multiply mode).

5

RECOMPOSING PHOTOGRAPHS

RESHAPING THE VIEW AND PERSPECTIVE

FRAMING THE IMAGE

CROPPING

How you crop a picture can make a huge difference to the way it is viewed and the strength of the composition. Some photographers prefer to crop in camera. Using this approach can be a good discipline, but it limits you to the aspect ratio of the camera frame. It is certainly a good idea to tighten the crop as you shoot, as a common mistake beginners make is to stand too far away from their subject. In my view, though, it is always wise to leave some room at the margins to allow for alternative crops, ones that are not confined to the limits of the camera frame area. I come from a commercial photography background, where I learned how important it is to leave a little spare room in your photographs. This is because the client or art director may require a specific crop that fits a page layout or packaging design, where the photo has to have the flexibility to fit the layout rather than the layout fit the photograph. In these instances, the final composition may have to include room to place headlines or graphical elements that superimpose the image. Or, more likely, the photograph has to be able to adapt to different layout crops. So, while it is good to crop as much as you can in camera and you don't want to waste pixels when cropping, it is wise to leave a little breathing room with which to refine the cropping at a later stage. Certain rules help explain why some compositions work better than others. The rule of thirds is where the frame is divided up into nine equal-sized segments. **Figure 5.1** shows a classic example of this type of composition. You can also look for symmetry, or align elements in a scene with the golden mean. Rather than analyze things too much, I suggest you go through your own work and make instant hit-or-miss judgments as to which ones work and which don't. Then take a closer look at the ones you liked and see if you can spot a pattern. You may find photographs that obey the classic rules of composition, but in general you will find the photographs that work best are those that one way or another communicate clearly. Good composition is essentially about emphasizing what's interesting and cutting the dross.

A useful rule is to make sure every bit of the picture counts. In Figure 5.1 there was a lot of empty space in the top and bottom thirds, but this helped balance the contents of the middle horizontal third. So although these areas are mostly blank, they serve an important purpose. If, on the other hand, I had included lots more sky or sea, the composition would have been unbalanced and overwhelmed with empty space. A bad composition is like a dull movie, where it takes forever to establish the plot, or for you to find any sympathy with the main characters. If a photograph contains distracting or irrelevant detail, it won't communicate as well as a photograph that immediately engages with the viewer. It's all about the editing and making your photographs stand out and be noticed. **Figure 5.2** shows how I was able to apply different crops to a full-frame image. In each example I tried to find different ways to crop the image and aimed to cut out distracting elements, such as the top of the building in the foreground, the shadows of the buildings, or signposts. At the same time, I looked to find interesting shapes within each frame. Notice how the bottom image matches the proportions of the golden mean spiral Lightroom crop overlay guide.

FIGURE 5.1 An example of a photograph that fits a rule of thirds composition.

FIGURE 5.2 The full frame image (top left) plus cropped variations.

FIGURE 5.3 The Crop Overlay tool panel controls.

As Shot
Original
✓ Custom

1 x 1
4 x 5 / 8 x 10
8.5 x 11
5 x 7
2 x 3 / 4 x 6

4 x 3   1024 x 768
16 x 9   1920 x 1080
16 x 10   1280 x 800

Enter Custom...

4.5 x 3.5
10.4 x 18.90

FIGURE 5.4 The Crop Overlay Aspect menu options.

The Lightroom Crop Overlay tool

The Crop Overlay tool options are shown in **Figure 5.3**. The simplest way to use this tool is to make sure the lock icon is set to unlocked mode and click and drag to define the desired crop of the image. As you click and drag on the preview, this moves the image relative to the crop, and if you mouse down or near the crop overlay handles, you can adjust the size, scale, or rotation of the crop. The Aspect menu (**Figure 5.4**) can be used to select custom aspect ratio settings or to create your own. So, if you wanted to apply a crop that specifically matched a 16:9 aspect ratio, you would select the 16 x 9 setting to constrain the crop overlay to those proportions. To straighten an image, you can click on the Auto button. This is effectively the same as applying a Level Upright adjustment (see "Upright adjustments"). Alternatively, you can drag the Angle slider to straighten an image, or select the Straighten tool to undock it and drag across the image to define the angle to straighten to. Checking the Constrain to Image option restricts the bounds of the crop to nontransparent pixels only. This applies to images that have transparent edges, such as those that have been modified using a Lens Corrections panel Upright or Manual adjustment. The Toolbar, which appears just below the Develop module image preview (press T to show/hide), has a Tool Overlay menu. When it's enabled, you can repeatedly press the O key to cycle through the overlay options, such as the one shown in the bottom image example in Figure 5.2.

ANGLE OF VIEW

The trickiest decisions you have to make are the viewpoint and timing of your photograph. While you can use dodge and burn techniques to improve the lightness and tonal balance, there is a limit to how much you can do in postprocessing to change the composition. Yet, as you will learn in this chapter, there are a few tricks that can be employed to make it appear that a photograph has been shot from a different viewpoint. I show these partly so that you can learn how to apply such techniques to your own photographs, but also as a way to teach about composition and the art of aligning the elements in a scene to achieve a strong composition.

CONTENT-AWARE SCALE ADJUSTMENTS

A really effective way to alter the composition in a photograph and change the apparent angle of view is to use the Content-Aware Scale feature in Photoshop. This can be used to automatically detect which are the most important elements in an image and allows you to rescale (squash or stretch) the proportions of the image to change the aspect ratio and have the important elements remain unstretched. The best way to explain this is with the following step-by-step example, in which I tightened up the composition.

Compressing the elements together

This photograph has a lot of potential with engaging content. As the photographer, Richard Eyers, explains: "This image was captured on a Fuji X20 camera and processed in Lightroom. The scene was a children's party in Nigeria, where the children had all run inside because of the rain, leaving behind a rather damp Mickey, with an abandoned pair of shoes and solitary balloon."

When you look at the original image, the individual key elements are rather isolated and the main subject is some distance from the camera. The following steps show how I recomposed everything to fit within a classic square format crop. If this photograph had been taken from an angle more to the right and with a slightly longer lens, a fairly similar result could have been achieved through choosing a different viewpoint, and very little extra Photoshop work would have been required.

1 In this photograph, some things were visually interesting and others were distracting. It was an image that had a lot of potential, making it worth manipulating the composition just a little to improve the arrangement of the main elements.

2 I wanted to step back a bit and analyze the elements in this scene and think how they could have been arranged better. The photograph was shot from position A using a wide-angle lens. As a result of this, the key elements, such as Mickey Mouse, the playhouse, the shoes, and the balloon all ended up looking a little lost. There was also quite a gap between the playhouse and Mickey. Now, imagine the photograph had been taken from position B, from an angle that was farther to the right and also with a slightly longer lens. A viewpoint like this would help align these elements so that they appeared closer together. By using the Content-Aware Scale feature in Photoshop, it was possible to simulate shooting from a different viewpoint.

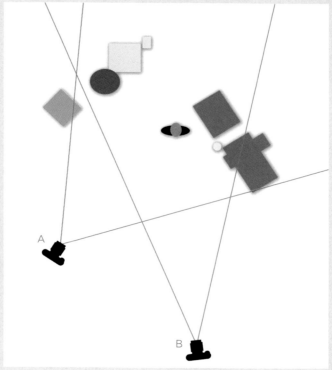

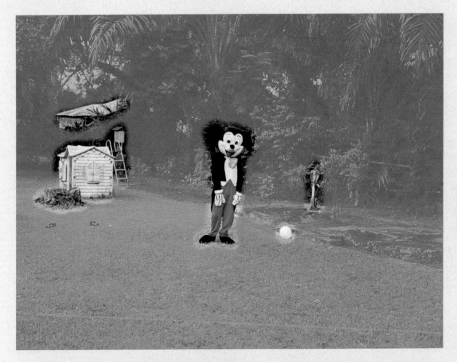

3 I opened the photo in Photoshop. To prepare the image for a Content-Aware Scale transform, I created a new alpha channel in the Channels panel, and with the channel mask visible and filled with black, I painted over the most important areas in white. This defined the parts I wished to protect from being scaled.

X: 700.00 px △ Y: 525.00 px W: 100.00% ∞ H: 100.00% Amount: 100% ∨ Protect: Alpha 1 ∨ ⊘ ✓

4 With the Background layer converted to an ordinary Layer 0, I selected Content-Aware Scale from the Edit menu. In the Options bar I selected the Alpha 1 channel from the Protect menu and checked the Protect Skintones option. I then dragged the right handle inward to squeeze the selected elements closer together.

5 I clicked OK to accept the Content-Aware Scale transform. I then selected the Crop tool and applied a square crop to produce the finished version image shown here.

Content-Aware Scale controls

The Content-Aware Scale feature allows you to recompose the aspect ratio of a photograph to stretch it horizontally or vertically and have key elements within the frame adjust their position without becoming distorted. It is an effective tool for reshaping a photograph to suit different layouts, but there are limits to how much you can stretch a photograph and still preserve the integrity of its contents. The edge detection that is employed is particularly good at recognizing what and what not to stretch. Where this breaks down, there are a couple of things you can do. In the Content-Aware Scale toolbar, there is a Protect Skin tones option (circled in **Figure 5.5**). When this is enabled, it improves the effectiveness of the edge detection so that skin tone subjects are protected more. In fact, it does more than recognize skin tones—it actually helps protect any recognizable shape from becoming distorted as you scale the image. The downside is that when enabled, the feature may deem too many elements in need of protection, thereby inhibiting the ability to scale effectively.

A more accurate protection method is to create a new alpha channel and paint on the mask with black to define the areas you wish to scale and paint with white to define the areas you wish to protect (as was shown in Step 3 in the previous example). You can then choose to load the alpha channel via the Protect menu in the Content-Aware Scale toolbar and then proceed to scale the image. Or, you can invert the mask to do the opposite and use the mask to define the areas you deliberately wish to see vanish as you rescale to make an image narrower.

The thing to watch out for as you apply a Content-Aware Scale adjustment is the jagged edges that appear where you squeeze parts of an image closer together, or obvious signs of stretching where the pixels are stretched farther apart. You do also have the option to use the Amount slider in the Toolbar. At 100% a full Content-Aware Scale is applied and at 0%, a full image transform is applied. This allows you to balance the amount of Content-Aware Scale that is used with a regular transform. Another thing you can do is to apply Content-Aware Scale in stages. As soon as you see signs of jagged artifacts or stretching, ease off slightly and confirm the adjustment. Then try applying the feature a second time and you may find you can continue to stretch or squash the image further without any of the key elements becoming distorted.

The following example shows how the Content-Aware Scale feature was used to enlarge the proportions of an image to add more space around the central subject in the photograph.

FIGURE 5.5 The Content-Aware Scale toolbar options.

Extending the canvas area

This photograph of a Cuban street sweeper was taken by Guy Pilkington. I especially liked the rich colors and the texture of the walls and doorway. My only criticism is that the composition could have benefited from having a bit more space on either side of the photograph. However, it is possible to use the Content-Aware Scale feature, as described below, to add more space on either side of the image without distorting the key areas of the image.

1 This shows the original version where the crop is quite tight, but there is the opportunity here to add more width to the picture.

Photograph: © Guy Pilkington

2 In this step I opened the JPEG original via Camera Raw. Using the Basic panel, I increased Exposure slightly and adjusted the Highlights and Shadows sliders. I also fine-tuned the Blacks slider to adjust the black clipping point and added a small amount of Clarity.

3 I then opened the image in Photoshop, where I double-clicked the Background layer to convert it to a regular Photoshop layer. Next, I selected the Crop tool and used this to expand the canvas size of the image, adding more space to the photograph left and right.

4 In the Channels panel I added a new Alpha 1 channel filled with black and painted the doorway area with white to roughly define it. After doing that, I clicked to select the RGB channel and turned off the visibility for the Alpha 1 channel.

Photograph: © Guy Pilkington

5 I then went to the Edit menu and selected Content-Aware Scale. This added a bound-ing box to the image that allowed me to stretch the image. Before doing this, I selected the Alpha 1 Channel from the Protect menu in the Toolbar. This ensured the doorway area remained unstretched as I dragged the side handles outward. Checking the Protect Skintones option also improved the quality of the scale adjustment.

FIGURE 5.6 The Lens Corrections panel Basic tab controls.

FIGURE 5.7 The Lens Corrections panel Manual tab controls.

UPRIGHT ADJUSTMENTS

The Lens Corrections panel contains Upright adjustment buttons that you can click to apply upright perspective corrections to an image (**Figure 5.6**). Upright adjustments are actually quite sophisticated, where the angle of view is recalculated taking into account the center of the new projection and how the rotation of one movement can affect another. You have four options to choose from—Auto, Level, Vertical, and Full—along with an Off button to reset adjustments. Upright adjustments are effective only when applied to photographs that contain straight lines; they have no effect on other types of images. Upright adjustments are therefore most useful for architectural photographs where you wish to correct the perspective. The best approach is to click on each of the four buttons to determine which of the Upright adjustments will have the best outcome.

The Upright options

The Level option is like an auto-straighten command and doesn't do anything more than attempt to straighten the edges to make them vertical or horizontal. The Vertical option combines a Level Upright adjustment with a converging verticals correction. The Full option combines a Level and Vertical Upright adjustment with a converging horizontal adjustment, which produces the most pronounced correction of all. Meanwhile, the Auto option combines all three types of Upright adjustments to produce a balanced combination, which at the same time avoids applying too strong a perspective correction.

Refining an adjustment

Whenever you click on one of the Upright buttons, it resets any crop that may have been applied to the photograph. It is therefore best to apply an Upright adjustment first before you crop the image. An Upright adjustment will change the shape of the image and therefore auto-crop the picture as an adjustment is applied. If you end up applying an extreme adjustment, you may see white padded areas at the edges of the frame (see Step 3 in the following example). You can remove these by manually applying a crop or by checking the Constrain Crop option. (I usually prefer to crop manually.)

An Upright adjustment that perfectly corrects the verticals can look a little odd. For this reason you may find it helps to click on the Manual tab (**Figure 5.7**) and set the Vertical slider to, say, +10 to make the verticals converge slightly. The manual controls also allow you to adjust the Distortion (which is a manual geometric distortion correction), adjust the convergence of the verticals and horizontals, and adjust the rotation. The Scale slider is useful if you need to reduce the scale and reveal areas that might have become cropped as a result of an Upright adjustment. Lastly, the Aspect slider can be used to compensate for the stretching or squashing of an image that may result from a perspective correction.

Applying an Upright adjustment

The following steps show how to apply an Upright adjustment and the additional steps you can take in Photoshop to fill in the transparent areas that can sometimes result from applying extreme Upright adjustments.

1 This photograph was taken of the billboards outside the Big Texan Steak Ranch in Amarillo, Texas.

2 I went to the Basic panel and applied a few tone and color adjustments to enhance the color and tone contrast.

3 In the Lens Corrections panel, I checked the Enable Profile Corrections and Remove Chromatic Aberration options. I also clicked the Full Upright button to apply an extreme perspective correction.

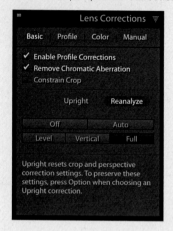

4 The above Upright correction distorted the image and resulted in transparent areas that needed to be filled in. I opened the image in Photoshop and selected the Clone Stamp tool to clone the grass. To fill in the sky I made a Magic Wand selection of the top left corner. I then chose Select ⇨ Modify ⇨ Expand to expand the selection by 10 pixels. I followed this by choosing Edit ⇨ Fill and filled using the Content-Aware method with the Color Adaptation option deselected.

5 This shows what the photo looked like after applying the Content-Aware fill in Step 4. Because the Color Adaptation option was unchecked, this filled the empty area with cloud detail similar to the rest of the sky. If the sky area you are filling is a cloudless blue sky, then it is best to have the Color Adaptation option checked.

6 The final step was to crop the photograph to narrow to a widescreen format crop that matched the proportions of the billboard display.

THE ADAPTIVE WIDE ANGLE FILTER

The Lens Corrections panel can be used to apply lens profile corrections to remedy geometric distortion. This can correct for curvature of straight lines, including photographs shot with a fisheye lens. Such corrections are global, which means the correction maps the entire frame area, reshaping it based on knowledge of the geometric distortion characteristics of each lens. While this can often help produce better-looking images, photographs shot using a wide-angle lens can sometimes benefit from selective perspective correction. This is because even when you correct for geometric distortion, objects toward the edges of the frame can appear elongated and round objects appear egg-shaped. This is where the Adaptive Wide Angle filter can be useful, as it allows you to selectively correct the perspective.

In this example, I photographed the Glenfinnan Monument using a 14 mm lens on a full-frame dSLR and had to tilt the lens up slightly to include all of the tower. By making use of the Adaptive Wide Angle filter controls, I was able to correct the converging verticals and ensure the walls and tower edges were all kept perfectly straight. The Adaptive Wide Angle filter adjustment produced a unique perspective correction of the monument. But because I didn't correct the top and bottom sections, this has created the impression the viewpoint is closer than it was in the original.

1 This shows the original photograph, which was shot with a 14 mm rectilinear lens using a full-frame dSLR sensor. I imported this photo into Lightroom, where I applied an Auto Basic panel adjustment and left Enable Profile Corrections unchecked in the Lens Corrections panel.

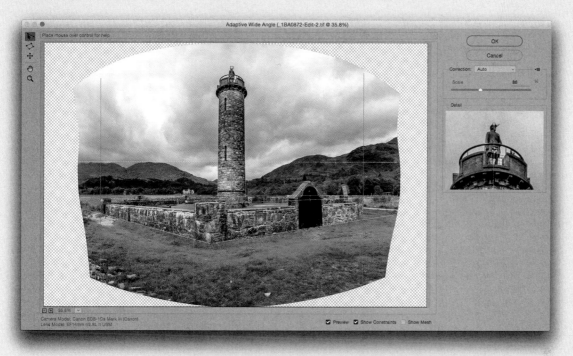

2 I went to the Photo menu and chose Edit In ⇨ Adobe Photoshop, where, from the Filter menu, I selected the Adaptive Wide Angle filter. With the Constraint tool selected, I added constraints to indicate which lines in the image should be made straight (these were colored cyan). For those that needed to be absolutely straight, I held down the ⇧Shift key as I did so. These were indicated with purple for the vertical lines and yellow for the horizontal lines. I also reduced the scale slightly before clicking OK to process.

3 Here is the final version, where I cropped the photo and filled in the four corners with a Content-Aware fill, using the same method that was described in the previous series of steps.

Removing elliptical distortion

1 This photograph was shot using a 14 mm lens on a full-frame dSLR camera. Because of the wide angle, the bicycle wheel appeared as a stretched, elliptical shape.

2 In this step, I went to the Lens Corrections panel, where I checked Enable Profile Corrections and selected the Vertical Upright adjustment to improve the perspective on the buildings. However, this happened to make the wheel distortion even worse.

3 I chose to undo the correction in Step 2 and reverted to the Step 1 state. I went to the Photo menu and chose Edit In ⇨ Adobe Photoshop, where, from the Filter menu, I selected the Adaptive Wide Angle filter. Here, I selected the Perspective Correction method and added a number of vertical, horizontal, and regular constraint lines to correct the straight lines. I then selected the Polygon Constraint tool to define the shape of the bicycle wheel and clicked OK.

4 In the previous step, I was able to selectively correct the perspective for the architectural lines and the bicycle wheel. I deliberately left the bottom section (apart from the wheel) uncorrected to maintain the wide-angle distortion. Finally, I made a selection of the bottom left and right areas and filled using the Content-Aware fill method.

TIP

It is a good idea to convert the image to a Smart filter first before you apply the Adaptive Wide Angle filter. This way you can go back and re-edit the settings at any time.

NOTE

The Puppet Warp feature is available from the Photoshop Edit menu and allows you to apply custom warps to images.

Adaptive Wide Angle filter controls

As you have seen in the two previous examples, the Adaptive Wide Angle filter can be very effective at selectively correcting the perspective. The initial dialog preview will vary depending on whether the underlying correction used is Auto, Perspective, or Fisheye. In most instances the Auto correction is automatically selected. Instead of applying a geometrically correct perspective correction, this applies a "shape conformal" projection, where the emphasis is on preserving the shapes in the image proportional to the distance from the viewer. To understand the key difference here, a lens profile correction in Lightroom, or the Lens Correction filter in Photoshop, will apply a correction where priority is given to obtaining the correct geometry at the expense of distortion in the way the image is projected. When using the Adaptive Wide Angle filter, priority is given to keeping the relationship between the elements in the scene in proportion, at the expense of being geometrically incorrect.

To use the Adaptive Wide Angle filter effectively, it is best not to apply a lens profile correction before you apply the Adaptive Wide Angle filter (especially if you are editing a fisheye lens image). A "shape conformal" projection is the starting point upon which you can add multiple constraints to determine which areas need to appear in "correct perspective." As you add constraints, you are effectively overriding the initial, selected projection and adding a perspective type projection to that particular section of the image.

The Adaptive Wide Angle filter works its magic by reading the camera body and lens EXIF metadata. It is then able to reference the lens profile database, allowing you to apply a geometrically correct perspective correction by adding constraints. As you do this it uses a Puppet Warp method to stretch or squash the pixels between the constraint lines. You can edit the constraints by clicking to select them and adjusting the endpoints. You can adjust the rotation as well, which can be useful if, say, you initially correct the lines of a building to make them vertical and then want to edit the lines to make the verticals converge slightly by a few degrees.

Photo merge corrections

The Adaptive Wide Angle filter is particularly good at correcting photo merge images, whether these have been created in Photoshop using the Photomerge feature or in Lightroom using the Photo Merge ⇨ Panorama method. As with regular images, the filter reads in the lens profile data and takes into account the warping that occurs when the images are merged together. This means as you add constraint lines, the filter will know precisely how to follow the lines of curvature distortion to correct the curved edges and make them appear straight. The Adaptive Wide Angle filter can do a really good job of improving the look of panorama images that have been created using a photo merge technique.

Correcting the perspective in a Photo Merge panorama

1 To create this Photo Merge panorama image, I began by selecting 10 single images in Lightroom and chose Photo ⇨ Photo Merge ⇨ Panorama (I explain this process in more detail in the following chapter). This produced the panorama image you can see here, where the images were all blended together smoothly, but the vertical and horizontal lines needed to be better aligned.

2 I opened the image in Photoshop and applied the Adaptive Wide Angle filter. This defaulted to the Perspective mode, where I added the constraint lines shown here.

3 I was then able to edit the Focal Length setting to change the apparent lens focal length from 10.4 mm to 20.8 mm. This made the image appear less "wide angle."

Expand Selection

Expand By: 10   pixels   OK

☐ Apply effect at canvas bounds   Cancel

4 After clicking OK to the Adaptive Wide Angle adjustments that were applied in Steps 3 and 4, I made a Magic Wand selection of the outer transparent areas. I then went to the Select menu and chose Modify ➩ Expand, where I expanded by 10 pixels. I followed this by choosing Edit ➩ Fill and applied a Content-Aware fill to the selected areas.

5 I saved the image in Photoshop so that I could carry on editing it in Lightroom, where I applied a few Basic panel tone and color adjustments to improve the contrast and color saturation.

6

BLENDING MULTIPLE IMAGES

MERGING MANY IMAGES INTO ONE

MERGING PHOTOS

With photography you often get only one chance to capture everything, which is why it is important to develop your technical skills to know how to be prepared for all eventualities. For those situations where you have time to work on getting the capture right, there is a lot to be said for shooting multiple exposures with a view to applying blending techniques at the postprocessing stage. In this chapter, we are going to look at ways you can use Lightroom and Photoshop to process multiple images and expand the processing potential of your photographs. As a colleague of mine, Jeff Schewe, once said to me on a road trip we took together, "You may only visit a place once in your lifetime, but you've got a lifetime left to process the photos you've shot." In other words, it makes sense to capture the hell out of any situation and give yourself options to do all kinds of cool stuff later.

You could call this type of capture "the indecisive moment," because you are basically hedging your bets by shooting lots of photos with the possibility of merging the best bits into one final image. For example, you can bracket the exposures at the time of capture to extend the dynamic range. You can pan the camera and shoot multiple exposures with a view to building a panoramic image, or combine this with bracketed exposure shooting to create a high dynamic range panorama. By simply taking lots of shots, you can use basic or advanced blending techniques to merge the best parts together to create an optimum composite. Or, you can bracket the focus to extend the depth of field. We'll begin with an example where I used a stack mode processing technique to combine multiple exposures of a tree and blend the dappled lighting from each exposure.

STACK MODE PROCESSING

The tree in this picture is one I have regularly passed on walks through our local forest, and I recently decided to spend some time photographing it. I set the camera up on a tripod and hung around for half an hour or so, repeatedly taking photographs whenever the dappled light hitting the tree looked interesting. I did so with the intention of combining all the shots into a single image. Needless to say, to create a photograph like this you need to have a reliable, sturdy tripod so the camera doesn't move between exposures, plus a little patience.

The method shown here relies on the use of smart objects and what's known as stack mode processing. Now, I should point out that the ability to create smart objects has until recently been limited to the extended versions of Photoshop. But this feature is now available to all Photoshop CC customers. If you don't have access to smart objects in Photoshop, you can still achieve the same kind of result by manually setting each layer and setting the layer blending mode to Lighten. It takes a little longer doing it this way, but the end result is more or less the same as using the Maximum stack blend mode.

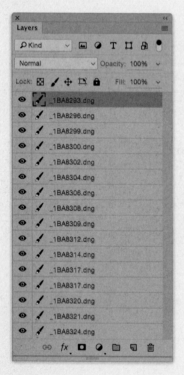

1 I selected the 18 source photos in Lightroom and went to the Photo menu, where I chose Edit in ⇨ Open as Layers in Photoshop. This created a new Photoshop document in which the selected images appeared as stacked layers in the Layers panel.

2 To prepare the image for the next stage, I needed to select all the layers. The shortcut for this is to use ⌘ Alt A (Mac), Control Alt A (PC). I then chose Layer ⇨ Smart Objects ⇨ Convert to Smart Object.

3 Next, I went to the Layer menu and chose ⇨ Smart Objects ⇨ Stack Mode ⇨ Mean. This processed the layers within the smart object to produce the flat contrast image shown here.

4 With the smart object layer selected, I chose Layer ▷ New ▷ Layer Via Copy. Now, with the copy smart object layer selected in the Layers panel, I chose Layer ▷ Smart Objects ▷ Stack Mode ▷ Maximum. This processed the layers within the smart object to produce a version that blended the dappled lighting effect from all the selected images.

5 In this step, I added a layer mask to the upper smart object layer, which was filled with black. Next, I changed the layer blend mode to Luminosity, selected the Brush tool, and with white as the foreground color began painting on the layer mask to selectively reveal the dappled light effect on the tree trunk and foreground.

6 One consequence of this technique was that the tree leaves in the background looked slightly blurred. In this step, I opened a single image from the original sequence and added it as a new layer. I then added a layer mask filled with black and painted with white to reveal the trees and leaves in the background. To darken the background, I added a Curves adjustment layer that dulled down the highlights. I then painted on the adjustment layer mask to hide the tree trunk and foreground areas.

7 Lastly, I saved the layered image so that it was automatically added to the Lightroom catalog. Back in Lightroom I converted the photo to black and white, added a sepia split tone effect, and added a darkening vignette.

CREATING HDR IMAGES

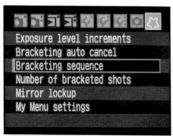

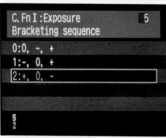

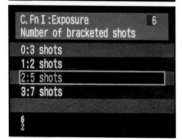

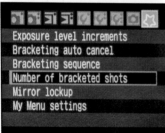

FIGURE 6.1 The bracketed expo-sure settings options for a Canon EOS camera.

The best way to extend the dynamic range of your sensor is to shoot a bracketed sequence of photographs and merge these together using High Dynamic Range (HDR) processing. There are various ways you can do this. You can use a third-party program such as Photomatix Pro; there is the Merge to HDR Pro feature in Photo-shop, and now an HDR Photo Merge feature has been added to Lightroom. I have used Photomatix Pro in the past and generally found the controls easy to work with compared with working with Merge to HDR Pro in Photoshop. In my view, the Lightroom HDR Photo Merge method is convenient because you can don't need to go out to Photoshop to apply the HDR processing. Best of all, the processed image is output as a DNG. This is created directly from the raw data in the original files, rather than going through an in-between step to convert the file data to integer pixel data first before you can create a floating point master. Another big plus is you get to use the familiar Develop panel controls when processing HDR DNG images.

HDR shooting tips

To create an HDR image, you will need to shoot a bracketed sequence of two or more images, adjusting the exposure by two stops for each capture. Your camera may well have menu controls that allow you to enable bracketed shooting, where you can configure the exposure difference and number of shots in an HDR sequence (**Figure 6.1**). Once the bracketing mode has been enabled, you just have to keep pressing the shutter to capture the three or five shots in quick succession. It is pos-sible to get good results when hand-holding the camera, but ideally you want to have the camera on a tripod. When setting up the camera to shoot an HDR sequence, make sure autofocus is disabled and focus manually. The camera metering mode should be set to manual and the lens aperture remain fixed. This is because when you shoot a bracketed sequence, the lens aperture (and therefore the depth of field) must be the same throughout.

When processing a bracketed sequence of images using the HDR Photo Merge feature in Lightroom, you can get great results merging just two images together. Otherwise it is recommended you shoot a sequence of three, five, or seven images. In most situations, three images at two stops apart on either side of the "normal" exposure should be enough to capture a wide dynamic range scene.

One of the things you have to appreciate is that photographers who shot negative film always had the ability to capture a wide dynamic range of tones. This was also dependent on how the film was exposed and developed. At the darkroom print stage, you could choose an appropriate contrast grade of printing paper and selectively lighten or darken the image as necessary. In this respect, you can say there is nothing necessarily new about HDR capture and HDR image processing. It's simply a digital technique that allows you to play with an extended tone range.

Creating an HDR Photo Merge in Lightroom

The Lightroom HDR Photo Merge feature makes it really easy to process two or more bracketed raw photos and merge them together to create a single, master HDR DNG image.

The photos below were taken at the iconic Cadillac Ranch. Created in 1974 by a group of artists known as the Ant Farm, it features 10 Cadillac cars half buried in a field just west of Amarillo, Texas, on historic Route 66. The art installation is just a short stroll from the car park, which is perfect for working off a 32-ounce steak from the local Big Texan Steak Ranch.

Considering their age, most of the Cadillacs have survived quite well, although some look like all that's holding them together is the graffiti spray paint. At the time I visited, the sun was up high in the sky, which created deep, harsh shadows. As you can see in the middle picture below, this was a tricky scene to photograph with just a single capture. The answer was to shoot a bracketed sequence of photographs where the exposure was made two stops lighter and darker on either side of the normal exposure. I was then able to use the HDR Photo Merge feature in Lightroom to blend the three raw photos together to produce a single HDR DNG that could be edited like a regular raw image in Lightroom. An HDR Photo Merge will produce a 16-bit floating point DNG (see **Figure 6.2**), where the range of the Exposure slider range will be increased to plus or minus 10 stops.

FIGURE 6.2 If the Metadata panel is set to show DNG information, HDR DNGs can be identified as having floating point pixel data and a bit depth of 16 bits.

1. I took three bracketed exposures of one of the Cadillac cars with two stops of exposure difference between each shot.

2. In Lightroom, I selected the three photos shown in Step 1 and chose Photo ⇨ Photo Merge ⇨ HDR. This opened the HDR Merge Preview dialog. As the photos I took were hand-held, I checked the Auto Align option and also checked the Auto Tone option. I left the Deghost option set to None, because there was no significant subject movement to take into account here. I was then ready to click Merge.

3 This shows the HDR Photo Merge image that was produced in Lightroom. Because the Auto Tone option had been checked in the HDR Merge Preview dialog, this applied an Auto Tone setting that I was then able to modify. When processing HDR images in Lightroom, it is often necessary to set the Highlights slider to -100 and the Shadows slider to +100. This combination of slider adjustments can leave the midtones looking rather flat. This can be overcome by adding more Clarity.

4 In the Basic panel White Balance (WB) section, I applied a cooling white balance setting to add more blue color to the sky. I then went to the Tone Curve panel and applied the tone curve shape shown to add more contrast in the shadow and highlight areas.

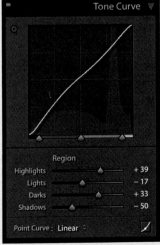

5 Finally, I added a Radial Filter adjustment to add more warmth to the middle of the image and lightened Exposure slightly. This provided a nice color contrast between the car and the surrounding area and made the graffiti painting stand out more.

CREATING A PANORAMA PHOTO MERGE

The Photomerge feature in Photoshop has been much improved over the years. As well as using Lightroom to create HDR photo merges, you can also create panorama photo merges, which are likewise saved as DNGs. This means if the source images are all raw files, a panorama DNG can be edited just as you would edit a regular raw image, with all the flexibility you would normally expect to extract detail in the shadows and highlights.

It helps, of course, if you capture the photos using a tripod, but even if you don't this shouldn't present too much difficulty when you create a panorama photo merge. The main thing to watch out for is the evenness of the exposures and to ensure you are able to retain all the tone information in the highlights and shadows in each capture. If this is likely to be a problem, you can always plan to shoot exposure bracketed images at each step, merge these using the HDR Photo Merge method, and edit the HDR DNGs to obtain the optimum tone output. After you have done that, you can select the edited HDR DNGs and build a panorama image using Photo Merge.

NOTE

Photoshop calls the panorama merge process Photomerge, while Lightroom describes it as Photo Merge.

1 Here, you can see three photographs that were shot as a panoramic sequence. I deliberately shot these at a slightly darker than normal exposure setting to ensure I preserved all the highlight detail in the sky.

2 With the three images selected in Lightroom, I went to the Photo menu in the Develop module and chose Photo Merge ⇨ Panorama. This opened the Panorama Merge Preview dialog. In this step, I checked the Auto Select Projection option, which in turn, selected the Spherical projection method. As this worked nicely, I proceeded to click the Merge button.

3 This created a panorama DNG image, which was automatically added to the Lightroom catalog in the same folder location as the source images. In the Develop module, I applied the Basic panel adjustments shown below to lighten the panorama photo and add more vibrance.

4 This shows the final edited version, which was cropped slightly to remove the overhanging branch in the top-left corner.

FIGURE 6.3 A 360° virtual reality tripod head.

Projection options

The Lightroom Panorama Photo Merge feature provides three projection options. The Spherical method is best for multirow panorama captures. The Cylindrical method is best suited to panoramas comprising a single row of images, while the Perspective method applies a straight, geometric projection. These options are good for merging a great many types of panoramas, and you do have the option to check the Auto Select Projection option and allow the Panorama Photo Merge to automatically choose the most appropriate one for you. However, the following step-by-step tutorial demonstrates how the regular Photoshop Photomerge feature can sometimes produce better-looking results.

PHOTOSHOP PHOTOMERGES

The Photomerge feature in Photoshop has been around for quite a while now and has undergone various refinements to produce more accurate stitches. To get the best results, the lens aperture should be consistent, and you need to ensure there is something like at least a 25% overlap between each exposure. As I mentioned earlier, the camera should ideally be mounted on a tripod, and to get the best results you might want to use a special virtual reality panorama head such as the one shown in **Figure 6.3**. This will allow you to accurately position the camera so that the nodal point of the lens is precisely aligned with the pan axis of rotation. This can help you avoid the parallax effect, where objects in the field of view appear to move relative to each other as you pan the camera. This is critically important if your aim is to produce a 360° spherical virtual reality image. For regular panorama stitches you don't need such precision, but the more you can do to get the camera to rotate around the lens nodal point, the more successful the stitch will be.

In the following example, I used the Photoshop Photomerge method to produce an extreme wide-angle Photomerge. Starting in Lightroom, I chose Photo ⇨ Edit In ⇨ Merge to Panorama in Photoshop. I configured the settings so the layers were blended together in the final Photomerge. Alternatively, you can carry out a Photomerge in gradual stages. To do this, go to the Photo menu and choose Edit In ⇨ Open as Layers in Photoshop. This creates a layered document in Photoshop. By going to the Image Size menu and reducing the pixel dimensions, you can limit the eventual panorama size and speed up the Photomerge processing. With all the layers selected, go to the Edit menu and choose Auto-Align Layers. This opens a dialog similar to the one shown in Step 2, where you can select the desired projection method. You can apply this and check to see the outcome of the panorama stitch. If you don't like the result, you can simply undo that step and repeat by selecting a different projection method instead. Once you are happy with a panorama projection, go to the Edit menu again and select the Auto-Blend Layers option, which will add layer masks to the selected layers to produce a finished panorama (as shown in Step 3).

An extreme wide-angle Photomerge

It used to be the case that wide-angle lens captures wouldn't stitch together so effectively. When I first started using this method, I would make sure the focal length of the lens was no wider than the equivalent of shooting with a 35 mm lens on a full-frame camera. Because of the way the Photomerge feature in Photoshop now uses the lens metadata in conjunction with the lens profile database, this does now allow wider-angle lens shots to be stitched more successfully. I find that the photomerge results you can achieve using an extreme wide-angle lens may look rather distorted, but this can be corrected by applying the Adaptive Wide Angle filter. Although this tool was primarily promoted for use in architectural photography, it is actually very effective when applied to landscape panorama subjects. The individual photographs I used to create this panorama were shot using a 14 mm prime lens on a full-frame dSLR. Using Photomerge and the Adaptive Wide Angle filter, it was possible to merge these together to produce a super-wide-angle view.

TIP

The Photoshop Photomerge process does have a tendency to cause the highlights and shadows to clip. For this reason, it is best to ensure the source images are flat in contrast with plenty of headroom at either end of the histogram. You can then optimize the color and contrast at the end.

1 To produce the following Photomerge image, I captured a panorama sweep of 15 separate photographs. These were all shot using a 14 mm wide-angle lens and photographed with the camera mounted on a regular tripod. As I shot this series of photographs, I aimed for a greater than 50% overlap between each exposure. Here, you can see I selected all the photos in Lightroom.

2 In Lightroom, I selected Photo ⇨ Edit in ⇨ Merge to Panorama in Photoshop. This opened the Photomerge dialog, where I selected the Auto projection option. At the bottom I checked Blend Images Together, Vignette Removal, and Geometric Distortion Correction. This created the panorama shown below with layer masks applied to each layer.

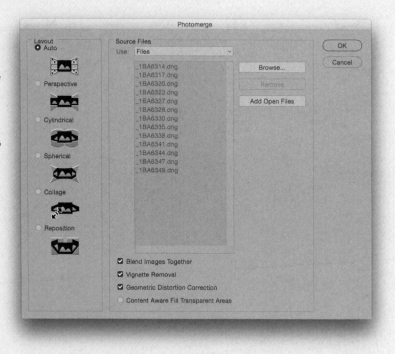

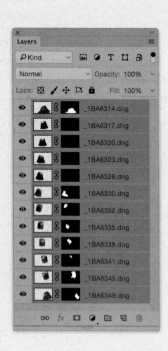

3 I went to the Layer menu and chose Flatten Image, after which I went to the Filter menu and chose Convert for Smart Filters. I applied the Adaptive Wide Angle filter, adding the constraints shown here to straighten the image, before clicking the OK button.

4 This shows the panorama image after I had applied the Adaptive Wide Angle filter and after I had cropped the image in Lightroom. Using the Basic panel in Lightroom, I added a few tone and color adjustments to produce the finished result.

5 The perspective appearance in this image clearly shows an ultrawide view, but at the same time it doesn't look too distorted.

BLENDING MULTIPLE FLASH EXPOSURES

The latest battery-powered flash units are powerful and versatile, but when you are shooting on location you need to travel as light as possible. One solution is to capture multiple exposures with the camera mounted on a tripod, where you can use a single flash head to light different areas of a scene. Having done that, you can merge the separate images in Photoshop to create a blended composite. The following example shows this technique applied to a portrait photograph I took of archaeologist Jonathan Hunn, where I photographed him on location at a derelict chapel. To get to this location, I had to carry all the required gear on foot for about half a mile, so it helped being able to travel light.

1 These are the four photographs that I shot with the camera on a tripod and merged together to create the final composite. I began by photographing my subject, Jonathan, concentrating on getting him in the right position and pose. I shot these using a portable flash head with a large soft box attachment, where the light was placed off-camera to the right. Afterward, I positioned the same light in three other locations and triggered the flash using a radio sync to light the derelict chapel from different positions.

2 To create the final version, I selected the four photos shown in Step 1 and in Lightroom chose Photo ⇨ Edit in ⇨ Open as Layers in Photoshop. This opened the files in Photoshop as a layered document. I then selected all the layers, went to the Photoshop Edit menu, and chose Auto Align Layers. If the camera had remained static on the tripod, it shouldn't have been necessary to do this. But when shooting lots of captures and with the camera tripod on unsteady ground, it is likely there will be some movement between exposures. I added an empty layer above the portrait image layer and used the Healing brush to remove a plant stalk from the foreground. I made Layer 2 visible (keeping Layer 3 and Layer 4 hidden) and Alt-clicked the Add Layer Mask button (circled) to add a layer mask filled with black. I then painted with white to reveal the lighting that was hitting the rear wall of the chapel. I repeated these same steps for the other two layers so the final composite looked as if it had been lit with multiple flash heads.

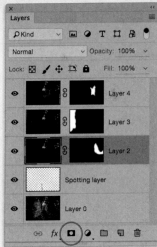

REMOVING STREET FURNITURE

It is not always possible to find a clear angle to take a photograph without something getting in the way of your shot. While you can wait till there are no cars or people in a scene, you are going to be stuck whenever lampposts or traffic lights obscure your view. Fortunately, you can get around such a problem by shooting multiple view-points and then merging these to remove unwanted foreground elements. All you have to do is take two or more shots from slightly different vantage points. I shot the photographs below about a meter apart, using the equivalent of a 28 mm lens on a full-frame camera (it is tricky to get this technique to work well if shooting with a lens with a wider angle of view than this). I then used Photoshop to align the photographs and applied a layer mask to remove the lamppost.

1 To start, I captured two photographs shot from slightly different viewpoints. It all depends on how much street furniture there is getting in the way of your view and the distance between it and the subject behind. In most situations, two photos should be all you need. In Lightroom, I went to the Photo menu and chose Edit in ⇨ Open as Layers in Photoshop.

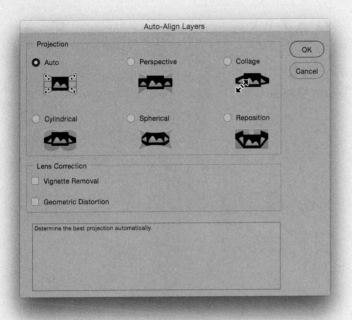

2 In Photoshop, I selected the two layers. I then went to the Edit menu and chose Align Layers. This opened the Auto-Align Layers dialog, where I selected the Auto Projection option. I left the two Lens Correction items unchecked and clicked OK.

3 The auto-align process aligned the selected layers without attempting to blend the photos. I was able to check the outcome of the auto-blend by turning the layer visibility of the top layer on and off. In this example, the alignment wasn't 100% perfect, but the lamppost could be seen to switch positions as I toggled the upper-layer visibility.

4 With the upper layer active, I
Alt-clicked the Add Layer Mask
button in the Layers panel. This
automatically filled the layer
mask with black and hid the layer
contents. By painting with white
on the layer mask, I was able to
selectively paint in the contents of
the top layer to hide the lamppost.

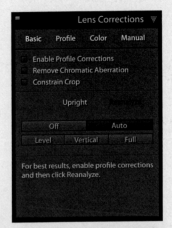

5 Once I was happy with the masking that had been applied in Step 4, I added a new empty layer to the top of the layer stack and retouched out the TV aerial on the roof. I then chose File ➾ Save to save the image and add it to the Lightroom catalog. In Lightroom, I went to the Lens Corrections panel, where I applied an Auto Upright correction. In the Basic panel, I lightened the Exposure slightly and added more Vibrance. Next, I added a darkening Post-Crop Vignetting effect via the Effects panel. Lastly, I selected the Graduated Filter tool, added a blue Tint adjustment to the sky, and added a lightening Graduated Filter adjustment to the side of the building.

LAYER BLEND MODES

When you work with layered images in Photoshop, there are lots of different blend modes for you to choose from. For example, the Multiply blend mode can be used to overlap layers, like placing one transparency photograph on top of another. The Screen blend mode can be used to lighten in a way that is similar to creating a double exposure in camera. Then there are other modes like Overlay, Soft Light, and Hard Light that multiply or screen the colors depending on the base-layer image content. The following tutorial shows how I was able to creatively merge images using the Lighten blend mode.

Merging fireworks photos

The objective here was to merge a series of firework photographs to create a single big firework display image. The source photos were all shot with the camera mounted on a tripod and the camera set to ISO 100 using an exposure of 4 seconds at f/9.0. By photographing the individual firework explosions at just the right exposure, I had the freedom to decide which specific exposures would work best when combining them to build a single composite image. To do this, I used the Lighten blend mode to blend the layers together. This allowed me to cumulatively merge the individual firework images. It would have been possible to blend more than just four images without this affecting the black night sky, but in this case four was enough to achieve the desired result.

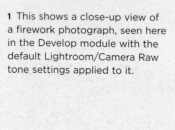

1 This shows a close-up view of a firework photograph, seen here in the Develop module with the default Lightroom/Camera Raw tone settings applied to it.

2 In the Basic panel, I set the Highlights slider to -62. This helped reveal more tone detail information in the firework trails. I also adjusted the Shadows, Whites, and Blacks sliders to achieve an optimum tone balance. I then went to the Presence section and added a +24 Clarity to boost the midtone contrast, which also added more detail to the firework trails. Next, I added +59 Vibrance to increase the color saturation.

3 I selected four images from the firework photos sequence and synchronized the Develop settings I had applied in Step 2 across all four photos.

4 I then went to the Photo menu in Lightroom and chose Edit in ⇨ Open as Layers in Photoshop. This generated a layered image, where the uppermost layer obscured the other three layers below.

5 I adjusted the layer blending modes for the top three layers, setting each to the Lighten blend mode. In this example, the second layer only was blended with the bottom layer.

6 In this step, you can see how the composite image looked with the top three layers all merged using the Lighten blend mode.

7 I merged all the layers in Step 6, added a new empty layer above the merged image layer, and used the Spot Healing brush (with Sample All Layers selected) to remove some of the unwanted light trails. I then added a couple of tree silhouette layers and set the blend mode for both of these layers to Multiply. This made it look as if the trees were in the foreground and helped frame the photograph.

FOCUS STACKING

Photoshop can be used to create focus-stacked images. While the Photoshop method described here may not equal the results of dedicated software such as Helicon Focus (Heliconsoft.com), it is still possible to get good results using the Photoshop method. The technique I describe here is especially useful for landscapes and some types of macro photography.

When you shoot a photograph, the depth of field is determined by a number of factors, such as the f-stop used as well as the focal length of the lens and also how close up you are focusing with that lens. The perception that a photograph has a wide depth of field is normally achieved by using short focal length lenses, such as a wide-angle lens, and/or stopping down the lens aperture. With the focus stacking technique, the idea is to shoot a series of photographs where you bracket the focusing for each capture and then use computer software (in this case, Photoshop) to blend the sharpest bits together to construct a picture in which everything appears sharp. This means if you shoot focus-bracketed photographs using a long focus lens, you can achieve a much greater depth of field than you would get normally.

The success of the depth-of-field blending technique comes down to the care with which you shoot the original photos. The more images you capture, the better the final quality. The key here is to adjust the focus in small, gradual steps. Some wireless camera control devices can be configured to adjust the lens focus in even, incremental steps. This can help automate the process when shooting a series of images from which to create a focus-stacked image. **Figure 6.4** shows the CamRanger iPhone interface that can be used to control the camera focus settings. This screenshot shows the focusing adjustment controls for setting up a stacked-focus shoot sequence.

FIGURE 6.4 The CamRanger device iPhone interface showing the Focus Stacking controls.

1 In Lightroom, I selected a group of focus-stacked photographs. I then went to the Photo menu and chose Edit In ⇨ Open as Layers in Photoshop.

2 This opened the nine selected photos as a multilayered image in Photoshop. With all the layers selected, I went to the Edit menu, chose Auto-Align Layers, and selected the Auto projection option. I left both of the Lens Correction options unchecked and clicked the OK button.

3 This aligned the layers, where each layer was focused on a different point within the scene. This screenshot shows the closest focus image. It was important to keep all the layers selected for the blending step that followed.

4 As you can see, when viewed in close-up detail, the house in the background appeared out of focus on this selected layer.

5 Here, you can see a close-up view of the same image layer, zoomed in on the bottom section, where the model tree in the foreground is in sharp focus.

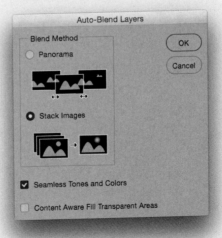

6 The next step was to merge the layered photos together, which I did by going to the Edit menu again. This time I selected Auto-Blend Layers. Here, I selected Stack Images and made sure the Seamless Tones and Colors option was also checked. To get the best results, it is important to carry out the Auto-Align step before you apply Auto-Blend.

Design and model by Hugo Hardy, Architect

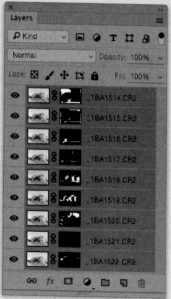

7 At this stage, the photograph appeared to be sharp all over, from the foreground to the background. Looking at the layer stack, you can see how, as a result of the Auto-Blend process, the individual image layers were all masked so that only the sharpest parts on each layer were made visible.

7
BLACK-AND-WHITE CONVERSIONS

SMART WAYS TO CONVERT YOUR IMAGES

FROM COLOR TO MONO

The best way to create black-and-white photographs is to capture your images in a raw format and carry out the color to black-and-white conversion in Lightroom. This gives you the ultimate flexibility to process the original raw color capture almost any way you like. All of this can be decided at the postediting stage, as opposed to choosing a black-and-white JPEG mode setting in the camera. The reason that is a bad idea is that the black-and-white conversion will then be fixed at the time of shooting. A similar argument can be made for professional cameras that have been designed to shoot in a raw black-and-white mode only. Again, you lose out on the ability to alter the color mix at the black-and-white conversion stage. The perceived advantage of these cameras, though, is that a single color channel sensor can capture more detail compared with a similar-sized Bayer pattern sensor, where the data from the four-color photosites has to be demosaiced to create a full-color image (which will then be converted back to black and white). However, when you consider the image quality you can get from a regular, high-resolution four-color sensor, the benefit is slight. What matters most is how you convert the color data to black and white. You can do this in Photoshop using a Black and White image adjustment, but I find the HSL/Color/B&W panel in Camera Raw and Lightroom is far more intuitive. This chapter demonstrates the main ways you can use Lightroom to convert color as well as showing you how to create a vintage-look photograph with a little help from Photoshop.

FIGURE 7.1 The HSL/Color/B&W panel controls.

1 This photograph was captured in color as a raw file and is shown here with the default Basic panel settings applied to it.

THE HSL/COLOR/B&W PANEL

To convert a color image to black and white, you can click on the Black & White button in the Basic panel, use the Ⓥ keyboard shortcut, or go to the HSL/Color/B&W panel (**Figure 7.1**) and click on the B&W button at the top. Whichever method you use, this applies a custom autoconversion that is linked to the White Balance settings. If you switch between the Basic and the HSL/Color/B&W panels, you will notice that each time you adjust the Temp and Tint sliders and convert from color to black and white, the default auto Black & White Mix slider settings will be different.

If you manually adjust the Black & White Mix sliders, you can decide how the grayscale information contained in the individual red, green, and blue color channels is mixed to create a black-and-white image. For example, if you drag the Red slider all the way to the right, this combines more information from the red channel relative to the green and blue channels and makes the red colors in the final black-and-white image appear lighter. If you drag the Green slider to the left, this will make the green colors appear darker. And, as you adjust the other sliders, you can make those colors, too, appear darker or lighter. If you click on the Target Adjustment tool (circled in Figure 7.1), you can click on the preview image to target the colors you wish to adjust. Drag upward to lighten and drag downward to darken.

2 In the Basic panel, I adjusted the White Balance (WB) to achieve a more natural-looking color. I then adjusted the Tone sliders to achieve an optimum tone balance for the color image.

3 In this step, I clicked on the Black & White button (circled) to convert the photograph from color to monochrome. This applied a default black-and-white conversion, which automatically adjusted the sliders in the HSL/Color/B&W panel.

4 In the Basic panel, I set the Clarity slider to +50. This increased the midtone contrast and enhanced the texture detail in the trees. In the HSL/Color/B&W panel, I selected the Target Adjustment tool, clicked on the tree trunks, and dragged downward to darken. I then clicked on the tree leaves and dragged upward to lighten.

5 Next, I selected the Graduated Filter tool and clicked near the top of the image and dragged downward to apply a darkening adjustment to the top half of the photo. I also added a further darkening Exposure Graduated Filter adjustment to the left side of the photo.

6 Finally, I went to the Split Toning panel and adjusted the sliders to add a sepia split tone coloring effect to the photograph.

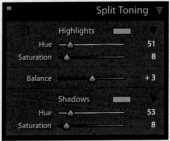

NOTE

The term split toning comes from a traditional black-and-white darkroom process, where through the use of multiple chemical baths, you could color the shadows and highlights separately.

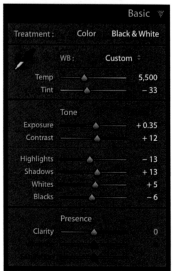

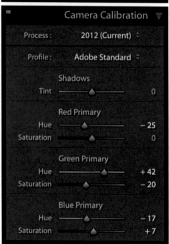

FIGURE 7.2 The key panels to use when making a black-and-white conversion.

ENHANCED BLACK-AND-WHITE EFFECTS

By adjusting the Black & White Mix sliders, you can produce all kinds of black-and-white looks, but there are other panels and slider adjustments that can affect the outcome of a black-and-white conversion. These are shown in **Figure 7.2**. As I mentioned earlier, the auto Black & White Mix adjustment is linked to the White Balance settings. It is therefore useful to have the Basic and HSL/Color/B&W panels open at the same time so you can easily switch between adjusting the Black & White Mix and the Temp and Tint sliders. For example, if you edit a scene that contains a lot of green foliage, setting the Tint slider to -150 will add a green cast that will cause the underlying green colors in a scene to appear much lighter. This type of adjustment can be used to create a pseudo black-and-white infrared film look.

However, when you push the Black & White Mix sliders to extremes, you can run into problems. For example, let's say you want to darken the blues and cyans to make a sky go darker. When you do this, there will first of all be the issue of noise. The blue channel is always the noisiest, and making a sky go darker will make any noise that's present more visible. Obviously, this is dependent on the quality of the original capture and how the image was exposed. The other thing to watch out for is the boundary between areas that have the greatest color contrast. Where you have, say, green trees outlined against a blue sky, darkening the blue sky or lightening the trees can result in a white halo around the border edge. If this happens, it is best to back off slightly with the Black & White Mix sliders and apply a less extreme adjustment.

Camera Calibration panel

If you can't get a sky to go dark enough, or you need the grass to appear lighter, the Camera Calibration panel can be used to modify Lightroom black-and-white conversions. You can do this by adjusting the Red Primary, Green Primary, and Blue Primary Hue and Saturation sliders.

Compared with the Black & White Mix controls, the Camera Calibration panel sliders are trickier to manage. This is because for each primary color, you have to find the optimum balance for the hue and saturation. This can mean a lot of going back and forth between all the sliders before you find an optimum setting. You will often find the outcome of these slider adjustments counterintuitive. For example, adjusting the Green Primary sliders can have a greater effect on a blue sky than adjusting the Blue Primary sliders. However, if you are prepared to spend a little time playing with these sliders, you can often achieve much smoother-looking black-and-white conversions as well as better tone contrast. The following example shows how I was able to improve the sky contrast in a landscape image.

1 I processed this image in Lightroom, where I used the Basic panel controls to optimize the tone exposure and contrast.

2 In this step, I went to the HSL/Color/B&W panel and clicked on the B&W button to convert the image to black and white. This applied an autoconversion based on the White Balance setting that was applied in the Basic panel.

3 To darken the sky, I selected the Target Adjustment tool (circled). I placed the cursor over the sky and clicked and dragged downward to darken. This modified the initial Black & White Mix settings and applied a negative Blue slider adjustment.

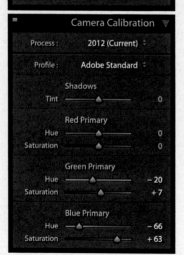

4 The Step 3 adjustment succeeded in darkening the sky, but it also ended up darkening the clouds. In this step, I eased off on the negative Blue adjustment and adjusted the Camera Calibration sliders to darken the sky, while preserving the cloud contrast.

5 In this final step, I went to the Split Toning panel and added a split tone adjustment that applied a warm color to the highlights and a cool color to the shadows. I kept the saturation low because I wanted this coloring effect to be kept subtle. To make the hue color temporarily appear more saturated, hold down the Alt key as you drag the Hue slider. This can help you visualize the final result without having to alter the delicate balance of the Saturation sliders. The middle Balance slider can be used to offset a split tone adjustment between the shadow and highlight colors. In this step, I set the Balance slider to +85. This meant that the split tone adjustment was more biased to the highlight color. Interestingly, even when the Hue slider settings are identical for both the highlights and shadows, the Balance slider can still have a subtle effect on the overall split tone effect.

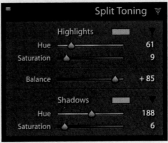

FIGURE 7.3 The HSL/Color/B&W panel in HSL mode with the Saturation tab selected and the sliders all set to -100.

TIP

To make the process easier, go to the Presets panel in the Develop module and save the above Color Adjustments settings as a new preset.

DESATURATED HSL ADJUSTMENTS

Another way to apply a black-and-white conversion is to use the HSL desaturation technique described here. Normally, when you convert to black and white, the Basic panel Vibrance and Saturation sliders are disabled. But if you use this method, they remain active and can be used to further modify a black-and-white conversion.

To carry out this type of conversion, you first need to go to the HSL/Color/ B&W panel (**Figure 7.3**), click on the Saturation tab, and set all the color sliders to -100. This converts the image to black and white and gives you full access to the controls shown in **Figure 7.4**. Basically, you can adjust the Luminance sliders in the HSL/Color/B&W panel the same way that you would the Black & White Mix sliders. You can also use the Target Adjustment tool to click and drag on the image to darken or lighten.

Having the Vibrance and Saturation sliders enabled provides you with more subtle control over a black-and-white conversion. Increasing the amount of Vibrance or Saturation will intensify the black-and-white conversion settings, and reducing the Vibrance or Saturation will mute them. This means you can use the Luminance sliders to achieve the desired color mix tone balance and then use, say, the Vibrance slider as an intensity slider with which to boost or suppress the overall effect. This is easier and a lot quicker than readjusting the individual sliders one by one.

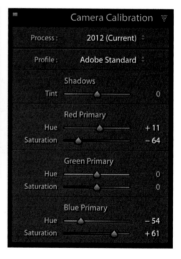

FIGURE 7.4 The panel controls for modifying an HSL desaturated black-and-white image.

1 The original photograph was shot on an early misty morning in a bluebell forest and was processed here using the default Basic panel settings.

2 I edited the Basic panel settings to add more contrast, where I mainly used the Whites and Blacks sliders to stretch the histogram to create a fuller tone range. I then applied the settings shown in Figure 7.3 to desaturate the image.

3 In the HSL/Color/B&W panel, I clicked on the Luminance tab and adjusted the sliders to apply a custom black-and-white conversion.

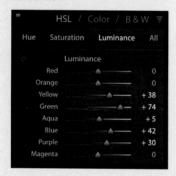

4 The colors in the original photograph were muted, so it helped to go back to the Basic panel and apply a +55 Vibrance adjustment to intensify the Luminance settings applied in Step 3. I also applied a +100 Clarity adjustment.

5 The combination of the Basic panel and HSL slider adjustments produced an enhanced black-and-white conversion in which the bluebells appeared lighter than they did in the default black-and-white conversion. Finally, I went to the Split Toning panel and applied a split tone effect that colored the shadows a green/blue color and the highlights a blue/magenta color.

NOTE

When you're adding and saving a graphical image as an Identity Plate preset, the Identity Plate Editor assumes you are creating a preset to replace the standard Lightroom identity plate logo that appears in the top-left corner. For this reason, you will see a warning dialog recommending you make the file smaller. You can safely ignore this if your intention is to use it as an overlay in the Print, Slideshow, or Web modules.

ADDING BORDER OVERLAYS

The Page panel in the Print Module has an Identity Plate section where, if you click on the arrow that's circled in **Figure 7.6**, you can select an identity plate to add as an overlay. If you choose Edit from the menu, this opens the Identity Plate Editor shown in **Figure 7.5**, where you can load a graphic, such as a high-resolution photographic border image. Figure 7.6 shows a Polaroid border image as it appeared in the Print preview, scaled using the Page panel controls.

FIGURE 7.5 The Identity Plate Editor dialog.

FIGURE 7.6 The Print module Page panel controls for adding a custom identity plate.

Creating a vintage black-and-white look

1 The original color portrait was processed in Lightroom to optimize the tone range.

2 Staying in the Basic panel, I clicked on the Black & White button at the top to convert the image to black and white. I adjusted the Exposure setting to make the photograph slightly brighter.

3 In this step, I opened the HSL/ Color/B&W panel and manually adjusted the Black & White Mix sliders. The objective here was to modify the color to black-and-white conversion and soften the tone contrast.

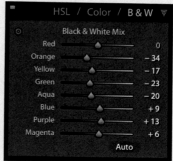

4 The camera lenses used in the 19th century tended to fall off in sharpness toward the edges of the frame. To replicate this, I added a Radial Filter adjustment, where I set the Sharpness to -100 and the Clarity to -48 and applied to the outside areas (shown here with a red overlay). I then right-mouse clicked on the Radial Filter adjustment pin and selected Duplicate to copy the adjustment in situ. This effectively doubled the negative Sharpness softening effect. You can do this perhaps once more to create an even softer result, but the degree of softening will diminish after the effect has been applied a couple of times.

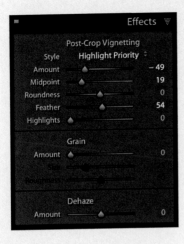

5 In the Effects panel, I added a Highlight Priority darkening Post-Crop Vignetting effect to darken the corners of the image. Having done that, I chose Photo ⇨ Edit in ⇨ Edit in Adobe Photoshop to prepare the image for the next stage.

6 Meanwhile, I located the two images shown here in Lightroom and chose Photo ⇨ Edit in ⇨ Edit in Adobe Photoshop. These were to be used as texture and color layers. The image on the left was sourced from the Lostandtaken. com website, where you can download a set of 11 different grungy-looking textured back-ground images in return for a donation (tinyurl.com/yl8fhhi).

7 In Photoshop, I took the black-and-white textured image and with the ⇧Shift key held down, dragged with the Move tool to place this as a layer above the portrait image layer. I renamed the texture layer Tintype and set the layer blend mode to Overlay. I also reduced Opacity to 68%. If you are doing this on one of your own images, you may want to add a layer mask to the textured image layer and paint with black to hide areas where the texture may obscure important areas of the photograph.

8 I then selected the colored texture image and again, with the ⇧Shift key held down, dragged with the Move tool to place this as a new layer at the top of the layer stack. Here, I set the layer blending mode to Color and set Opacity to 86%. This applied a tarnished color effect to the textured image.

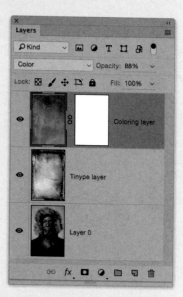

9 Having done that, I saved the image in Photoshop to automatically add it to the Lightroom catalog. Back in Lightroom, I selected the photo and in the Develop module went to the Split Toning panel. Here, I adjusted the sliders to add a sepia split tone effect to the final photograph.

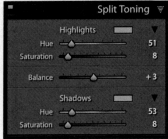

Photograph: © Eric Richmond

FIGURE 7.7 The Print module Print Job panel.

BLACK-AND-WHITE PRINT OUTPUT

Black-and-white printing is not much different from printing in color, except there are a few more options for you to consider. To print directly from Lightroom, go to the Print Job panel settings in the Print module (**Figure 7.7**) and configure the settings. In this particular example, I chose to make a print using an Ultra Smooth fine art paper on an Epson printer. Here, I enabled Print Sharpening, setting it to Standard, and selected Matte as the media type for the sharpening process (to match the fine art paper matte finish). Instead of managing the printing via the printer, I chose a preselected profile for the media I was printing to; the rendering Intent was set to Perceptual, which is usually the best to select when making black-and-white prints.

Output tone range

With black-and-white photographs, what matters most is the tone range. This will inevitably become compressed during the print process, especially if you are printing to a fine art matte paper. So although you don't have to worry about the color, it is still just as important to use soft proofing in the Develop module to see a preview of what the print will look like. By enabling the Soft Proofing preview, you can make further tone adjustments, which will prompt creating a virtual copy to save as a print setting version of the master image. Seeing a soft proof preview can guide you to refine the image's appearance. For example, a black-and-white photograph will appear to lose contrast when it's printed to a matte paper. This is because of the reduced tone range of the print output. To compensate for this, you can increase Clarity to boost the midtone contrast. Also, if, under normal print viewing conditions, there is a mismatch between the brightness of the preview on the display and the brightness of the print, it may be desirable to check the Print Adjustment button to apply a Brightness or Contrast adjustment.

Optimum quality and print longevity

Dedicated gray ink sets can be used in place of the regular color ink cartridges that are normally used with a printer. For example, Piezography K6 and K7 inks are compatible with a number of Epson Pro inkjet printers. These are available in different formulations to output to a select range of media types and require you to use a dedicated raster image processor (RIP). The advantage of this method is that it prints using gray inks of overlapping shade density rather than by varying the size of the ink droplets, which is what happens when you use a regular operating system print driver. Piezography also makes pure carbon inks. Prints made with these inks on the right media will, over time, fade less than 5 percent. This loss will be barely detectable and offers much better archive performance compared with regular color ink sets.

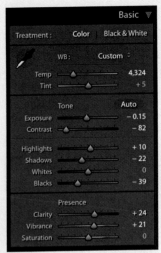

1 This color image was optimized in Lightroom to get the best tone and color balance for a color output. However, what looks nice in color won't always translate well to black and white when making a print output.

2 In this step, I clicked on the Black & White button in the Basic panel to convert to black and white. This automatically applied the Black & White Mix adjustment shown here, which was based on the current White Balance setting.

3 Next, I checked the Soft Proofing option to create a soft proof preview that used a fine art matte paper profile. I selected the Perceptual rendering intent and checked Simulate Paper & Ink. The proof preview showed that the image would print quite flat.

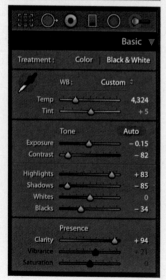

4 This is why it is important to soft proof. I adjusted the Black & White Mix sliders to achieve a better conversion. I also adjusted the Highlights and Shadows sliders in the Basic panel to add more global contrast and set the Clarity slider to +94. I could now print with confidence to the fine art matte paper selected in Step 3 and achieve a good print.

8

RETOUCHING

LIGHTROOM IMAGE MANIPULATION

PAINTING BY NUMBERS

Lightroom evolved out of Camera Raw as a raw processor and image management program. Early versions had a basic Spot Removal tool that could be used to carry out simple image retouching, but the performance was somewhat restrictive. To carry out any kind of serious editing, it was always necessary to export to Photoshop. These days, however, you can do more things exclusively in Lightroom. The current Spot Removal tool is noticeably faster and can be used to create brush spots as well as circle spots. When painting with the Adjustment brush, you have control over Opacity, Size, and Feather, plus Opacity can be adjusted by varying the amount of pen pressure that's applied using a Wacom tablet.

Essentially, the retouching work you do in Lightroom is saved as instructional edits to the file's metadata. You can retouch at any point in the image-editing workflow, and the edits you apply remain fully editable. This means you can revisit an image at any time and make further modifications to the Lightroom Develop module settings. For example, I have photographs in my Lightroom catalog that were edited some years ago using Process 2003. If I wish to update these to Process 2012, and add, say, a perspective correction, the previous Spot Removal edits will update automatically as I continue working in the Develop module. By contrast, if you export a rendered pixel image to edit in Photoshop, you are effectively editing a snapshot of the image settings at a fixed point in the image-editing process, and you'll have none of the flexibility that's offered by Lightroom.

FIGURE 8.1 The Spot Removal tool panel controls in Clone mode (top) and Heal mode (bottom).

SPOT REMOVAL TOOL

The Spot Removal tool (**Figure 8.1**) lets you nondestructively retouch photographs in Lightroom. You can remove dust spots and blemishes as well as larger, irregular shapes in Clone or Heal mode and have the ability to revise the adjustments you make or redo them completely.

Clicking with the Spot Removal tool creates a target circle spot and automatically selects the source area to clone from. Clicking and dragging creates a target brush spot and again, autoselects a source area with an identical shape to clone from (see **Figure 8.2**). Each circle spot you apply is represented by a circle spot overlay, and each brush spot is represented by a pin marker. You can hide these via the Tool Overlay menu in the toolbar or press the Ⓗ key to hide them.

Whether you click or drag, Lightroom automatically determines where best to sample from. If you are unhappy with an autoselection, you can press the Ⓘ key to sample a new area and keep doing so till you are pleased with the result. If that doesn't work and you wish to edit a circle spot or brush spot manually, you can click to select an individual overlay. This reveals the target and source, where you can click on the source spot or brush overlay and drag to locate a better source area. When applying circle spots, you also have the option of holding down the Ⓒⓜⓓ key (Mac) or Ⓒⓣⓡⓛ key (PC) and clicking and dragging to manually define the relationship between the target and the source.

FIGURE 8.2 This image had a mixture of circle spots and brush spots applied to it. The close-up views show a brush spot (left), where the thick shape outline was the target and the thin shape outline was the source, and a circle spot (right), where the thin circle was the target and the thick circle was the source.

Complex Spot Removal retouching

This photo of the Ta Prohm Temple in Angkor, Cambodia, was taken by Angela Di Martino. The original image was underexposed by about half a stop, but there was still enough detail in the highlights and shadows to fully optimize the important areas in this scene. The biggest problem was how to remove the unwanted elements such as the tourists at the bottom. One of the ways you can do this is to shoot a succession of images from the same viewpoint. You can then align these in Photoshop and remove the people from the scene through the use of layers masks. Or, you can use a Photoshop stack mode processing technique to do this automatically (see "Stack Mode Processing" in Chapter 6). In this instance, I relied on the power of the Spot Removal tool in Lightroom to remove the people and the overhead power cable.

1 To begin, I opened the JPEG original via Lightroom. Shown here is the image with the default Basic panel settings.

2 I lightened the Exposure setting and, at the same time, set Highlights to -100 to preserve as much of the cloud detail as possible. I then switched to the HSL/Color/B&W panel, where, in the Luminance section, I dragged the Blue slider to the left to darken the blue colors and add more contrast to the sky. I also darkened the green colors to reduce the halo edges around the tree leaves and dragged the Orange and Red sliders to the right to lighten the tree trunk.

3 This left the problem of what to do about the overhead cable and the people in the scene. I selected the Spot Removal tool and, in Heal mode, carefully brushed over the areas overlaid by the cable. I did this bit by bit in small steps. I clicked, held down the ⇧Shift key, and clicked again to create a straight brushstroke, connected between these two points.

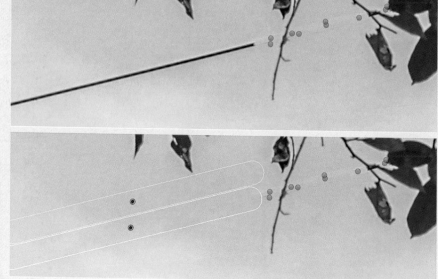

Basic

Treatment :	**Color**	Black & White
	WB :	As Shot
Temp		0
Tint		0

Tone — Auto

Exposure		+ 0.50
Contrast		− 9
Highlights		− 100
Shadows		+ 59
Whites		+ 20
Blacks		− 15

Presence

Clarity		+ 28
Vibrance		+ 24
Saturation		0

HSL / Color / B & W

Hue	Saturation	**Luminance**	All

Luminance

Red		0
Orange		+ 45
Yellow		− 38
Green		− 52
Aqua		0
Blue		− 40
Purple		− 1
Magenta		0

4 Here, you can see what the photograph looked like after I applied the Basic plus HSL/Color/B&W panel adjustments and removed the overhead cable.

5 To hide the people and other items at the bottom of the picture, I made further Spot Removal brush edits, again using the Heal mode.

Brush :		Clone	**Heal**
Size			21
Feather			55
Opacity			100
		Reset	Close

6 The trickiest bit was removing the two men who were in front of the tree roots. This required a lot of careful retouching work using the Spot Removal tool. To start with I used the tool in Clone mode to remove the men one section at a time. After that, I worked with the Spot removal tool in Heal mode to tidy up the clone mode retouching.

7 This shows the how the photograph looked with the people, posts, and rope barriers removed from the bottom of the picture. By this point I had added a lot of Spot Removal edits. As a result, the responsiveness of the Spot Removal tool had started to slow a little. This is the downside of doing a lot of heavy retouching work exclusively in Lightroom.

Photograph © Angela Di Martino

8 In the Tone Curve panel, I adjusted the curve shape to add more contrast in the highlights and lighten the shadow regions. Meanwhile, in the Effects panel, I added a darkening post-crop vignette. Because all the retouching work had been carried out in Lightroom, everything (including the Spot Removal tool adjustments) remained fully editable.

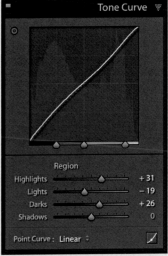

Tone Curve

Region		
Highlights		+ 31
Lights		− 19
Darks		+ 26
Shadows		0

Point Curve : Linear

Effects

Post-Crop Vignetting

Style	Highlight Priority	
Amount		− 9
Midpoint		45
Roundness		0
Feather		63
Highlights		0

Grain

Amount		0
Size		25
Roughness		50

Dehaze

Amount		0

NOTE

If you make Spot Removal edits by clicking to add circle spots or by dragging to add brush spots, these will be in an autoselect sample point mode and sync as described in the text. If you use the [Cmd] key (Mac), or [Ctrl] key (PC) and click and drag to manually define a circle spot's source point, the relationship between the target and source circle spot will be fixed when you sync the Spot Removal settings. Similarly, if you drag to create a brush spot and then manually adjust the position of the autoselected brush spot source, the relationship between the target and source will be fixed when you synchronize.

FIGURE 8.4 The Sync button in the Develop module has a switch to toggle between this and the Auto Sync mode.

Visualize Spots

When the Spot Removal tool is selected, you can select the Visualize Spots option in the toolbar, which is just below the Develop module image preview (**Figure 8.3**). When checked, this adds a threshold mode type of preview that is similar to the Masking slider threshold preview in the Detail panel. It enhances the edges in a photograph, and the slider control adjusts the threshold amount. This can make it easier to locate the sensor dust spot marks in a photograph.

FIGURE 8.3 The Visualize Spots option and slider control in the Develop module toolbar.

Syncing Spot Removal settings

Because the circle spot and brush spot edits are saved as metadata instructions, it is possible to synchronize the Spot Removal settings for one photo across many images. This can be beneficial if you have a lot of photographs that need spotting and they all share the same sensor dust spot marks. If you were to do all the retouching work in Photoshop, you would have to repeat the spotting work on every image. In Lightroom, you only need to retouch one photograph and the rest can be synchronized automatically. Furthermore, when you create a target circle spot or brush spot, this automatically selects the source to sample from based on an analysis of the surrounding image. When you sync the Spot Removal settings, you sync the target circle spots and brush spots only. Lightroom then autocalculates the sources for each separate image. In other words, the process is adaptive, and the selected sources will vary according to the image content.

There are two ways to sync images in Lightroom. One method is to make a selection of images and check the switch icon in the Sync button just below the Develop module panels (see **Figure 8.4**). In Auto Sync mode, the Develop module settings you apply are automatically synchronized with all the images in the selection. The other option is to edit one image first, make a selection of photographs, and click on the Sync button (Figure 8.4) to open the Synchronize Settings dialog to synchronize the Develop settings. The advantage of this method is you can choose precisely which Develop settings you wish to synchronize. The following steps show how I was able to use the Spot Removal tool to retouch one image and then synchronize the Spot Removal settings only with all the other photos in the selection.

Removing dust spots from multiple images

1 Here, I selected a set of nine seascape images that were all photographed over a couple of days using the same camera.

2 When the individual photographs were viewed close up, a lot of noticeable sensor dust spots needed to be removed. This shows a close-up view of the top-left corner of the first selected image.

3 To help identify the dust spots, I selected the Spot Removal tool and checked the Visualize Spots option in the Develop module toolbar. I was then able to drag the accompanying slider to adjust the mask threshold to make the dust spots visualization more apparent.

4 With the Spot Removal tool still selected, I applied circle spots to each of the identified dust spots, varying the size of the brush cursor as necessary. It is important to point out here that I did not manually set the circle spot source sample points.

5 This shows the photograph after all the dust spots were successfully removed.

Synchronize Settings

- ☐ White Balance

- ☐ Basic Tone
  - ☐ Exposure
  - ☐ Contrast
  - ☐ Highlights
  - ☐ Shadows
  - ☐ White Clipping
  - ☐ Black Clipping

- ☐ Tone Curve

- ☐ Clarity

- ☐ Sharpening

- ☐ Treatment (Color)

- ☐ Color
  - ☐ Saturation
  - ☐ Vibrance
  - ☐ Color Adjustments

- ☐ Split Toning

- ☐ Local Adjustments
  - ☐ Brush
  - ☐ Graduated Filters
  - ☐ Radial Filters

- ☐ Noise Reduction
  - ☐ Luminance
  - ☐ Color

- ☐ Lens Corrections
  - ☐ Lens Profile Corrections
  - ☐ Chromatic Aberration
  - ☐ Upright Mode
  - ☐ Upright Transforms
  - ☐ Transform
  - ☐ Lens Vignetting

- ☐ Effects
  - ☐ Post-Crop Vignetting
  - ☐ Grain
  - ☐ Dehaze

- ☐ Process Version ❗

- ☐ Calibration

- ☑ Spot Removal

- ☐ Crop
  - ☐ Straighten Angle
  - ☐ Aspect Ratio

❗ Settings that do not specify a process version may produce different visual results when they are transferred to photos with a different process version applied.

Check All   Check None   Cancel   Synchronize

6 Next, I made sure all the photographs in Step 1 were still selected in the Filmstrip and chose Settings ⇨ Sync Settings (or I could have clicked on the Sync button). This opened the Synchronize Settings dialog, where I checked the Spot Removal item only and clicked the Synchronize button at the bottom.

7 After synchronizing the Spot Removal settings, I selected one of the other photographs in the synchronized selection to check that the dust spots had been successfully removed. The synchronization process instructed Lightroom to apply Spot Removal edits to the exact same target spots as in the original, but to autoselect the optimum source spot areas on a per-image basis. Therefore, while the target spots were identical in each image, the source spots (the areas sampled from) were autoselected. In the above screenshot, you can see all the synchronized Spot Removal edit overlays.

RED EYE CORRECTIONS

The Red Eye Correction tool can be used to remove red eye from subjects when the flash was too close to the camera lens axis, resulting in the flash reflecting directly off the eyes' retinas to produce red-colored pupils. In Red Eye mode, you will see the cursor shown in **Figure 8.5**. To correct red eyes, place that cursor above the pupil, targeting the center with the crosshairs in the middle, and click (see **Figure 8.6**). This automatically applies a red eye adjustment that fits the size of the eye. Alternatively, you can click and drag with the tool from the center of the eye to define the area you wish to correct.

Pet Eye mode

If you photograph animals and the flash source is too close to the lens axis, you can end up with a problem similar to the red eye you get photographing human subjects. However, with animals, the retina reflections are rather different. Using Pet Eye mode you can similarly click on or drag from the center of the eye outward, to apply a correction and add artificial catchlights (see **Figure 8.7**).

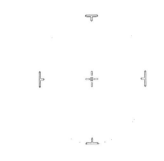

FIGURE 8.5 The Red Eye cursor.

 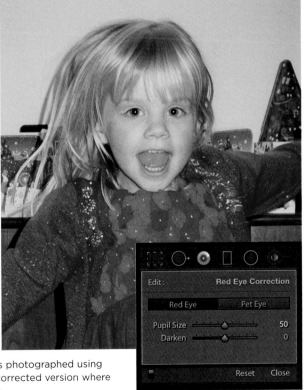

FIGURE 8.6 On the left is a before version where the subject was photographed using a compact digital camera with flash. On the right is a Red Eye–corrected version where the default settings were used to apply adjustments to each eye.

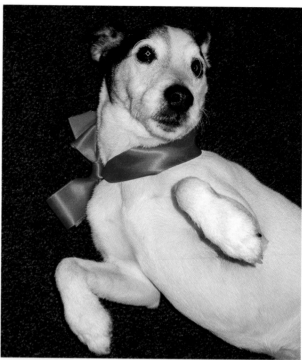

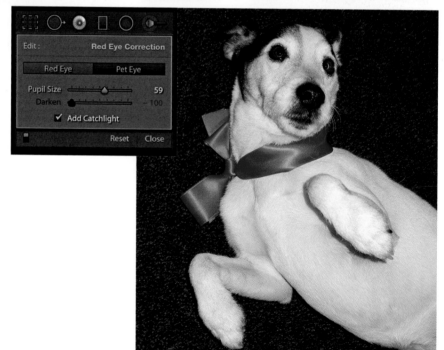

FIGURE 8.7 The top-left image shows a photograph of Biscuit, where the use of on-camera flash resulted in ghostly eye reflections. In the top-right example, I applied two Red Eye tool corrections in Pet Eye mode. The bottom image shows how these looked in the final version with the Add Catchlight option checked.

PORTRAIT RETOUCHING

Photoshop is the program of choice for complex image-editing work, but you can still do quite a lot to your photographs using the tools available in Lightroom. As was shown earlier, the Spot Removal tool can be used to retouch unwanted blemishes and remove objects. Such retouching can be refined by using lowered Opacity settings. For example, if you work with the Spot Removal tool using the settings shown in **Figure 8.8**, you can add circle or brush spots that suppress unwanted blemishes rather than totally eradicate them.

The Adjustment brush can be used to lighten or darken, but lots of other controls enable you to colorize, desaturate, or add contrast. The following steps show how I was able to use the Adjustment brush to selectively add negative Clarity. If you work with a pressure-sensitive tablet, such as a Wacom, you can use the pen pressure to control the brush Density.

FIGURE 8.8 The Spot Removal tool set to work with a lowered, 50% Opacity setting.

1 This photograph was taken in a studio setup and is shown here with the default Develop settings applied.

2 In the Basic panel, I adjusted the Tone sliders to improve the tone contrast.

3 In this step, I went to the Tone Curve panel and adjusted the tone Region and tone split Region sliders to darken the dark tones and add slightly more contrast to the highlights.

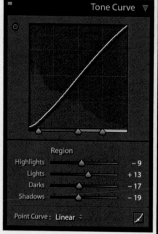

4 I then selected the Spot Removal tool and added a few brush spots to remove some of the loose hairs. To remove the skin blemishes, I set Opacity to 50% and added a brush spot in Heal mode that sampled from a source area of smooth skin tone.

5 I selected the Adjustment brush and set the Clarity slider to -100. I then painted carefully over the face to soften the skin tone texture, avoiding the lips and eyes.

6 The -100 Clarity adjustment made the skin look too soft, so I set the amount for this adjustment to -35. This revealed more of the original skin tone texture.

Client: Gallagher Horner, Model: Lucy Edwards @ M&P Models

HAND-COLORING PHOTOGRAPHS

In Chapter 4, I showed how you can use the Adjustment Brush to apply localized brushstrokes to modify an image. You can also use this tool to colorize photographs that have been converted to black and white. To do this, select the Adjustment brush, make sure the Auto Mask option is checked, and click on the color swatch to select a color to paint with. When you click on a target area in a photograph, this will sample the underlying color to create a selection mask that constrains the painting to the matching color areas only. I also find it helps to use the desaturated HSL adjustments technique discussed in Chapter 7 to carry out the black-and-white conversion. As you will see in the following example, this gives you the option to blend the original colors with the painted colors. This method also allows you to modify the Hue sliders in the HSL/Color/B&W panel.

1 Here, you can see a color version of the image I was about to hand-color. The following technique is most effective when working with color originals that have been converted to black and white in Lightroom, rather than starting out with a black-and-white original.

2 I converted the image to black and white by desaturating all the Saturation sliders in the HSL/Color/B&W panel and selected the Adjustment brush.

3 I clicked on the Color swatch and chose an orange shade with which to paint the wooden hut. I also checked Auto Mask. This allowed me to click on the hut and have Lightroom create a selection that limited the Adjustment brush painting to the underlying, color-matching areas only.

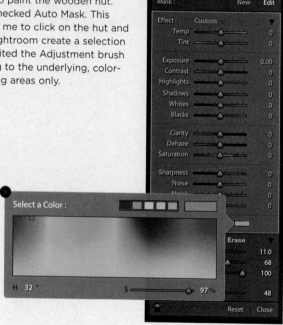

4 Next, I clicked the New button at the top and clicked on the trees in the picture to add a new Adjustment brush pin. I then clicked on the Color swatch and selected a lime green. With Auto Mask still checked, I painted over the trees to color the leaves.

5 I repeated the same steps as above, except this time I clicked on the sky area to add a new Adjustment brush pin and selected a blue color to paint the sky (I left the clouds unpainted).

6 In this step, I added a new Adjustment brush pin setting to the grass and painted with a blue-green color.

7 Next, I added a new Adjustment brush pin setting to the pathway and painted using a yellow color. I also painted over sections of the grass and the underside of the roof to add some color variation to these particular areas.

The following settings appear in the panels within the image:

HSL / Color / B & W

Hue | **Saturation** | Luminance | All

Saturation

Red	– 100
Orange	– 100
Yellow	– 87
Green	– 88
Aqua	– 100
Blue	– 85
Purple	– 100
Magenta	– 100

HSL / Color / B & W

Hue | Saturation | Luminance | All

Hue

Red	0
Orange	0
Yellow	0
Green	– 54
Aqua	0
Blue	– 62
Purple	0
Magenta	0

8 To create the final version shown here, I added a pin to color the building on the left and also reselected some of the other pins to mix the colors a little more. In Step 2, I had converted the image from color to black and white by setting the Saturation sliders to -100. This allowed me to readjust the Saturation slider settings by dialing some of the original color back in. For example, here I was able to restore small amounts of the Yellow, Green, and Blue saturation. I also adjusted the Green and Blue Hue sliders to modify the underlying color hue values.

SELECTIVE BLURRING

The miniaturization effect has proved popular in recent years and can be achieved in a number of ways. For example, you can create the effect in camera by photographing using a Lens Baby lens. This will allow you to capture the desired amount of blur and lens distortion at the time of shooting. An alternative option is to do this at the post-processing stage. For example, Photoshop CS6 saw the introduction of Blur Gallery filters, which include Field, Iris, and Tilt-Shift controls that can be used to apply lens blur effects. You can combine multiple filter adjustments and, in the case of the Tilt-Shift filter, apply different kinds of Distortion effects that closely match actual lens optical characteristics.

It is also possible to use localized adjustment tools in Camera Raw or Lightroom to apply negative sharpening effects, but you are restricted as to how much blurring can be applied using this method. In the example shown below, I created a panoramic image of a San Francisco nighttime scene and used a couple of Graduated Filter adjustments to apply negative sharpness blur effects at the top and bottom to mimic the effect of a tilted lens.

1 I selected the above four exposures in Lightroom and chose Photo ⇨ Photo Merge ⇨ Panorama.

2 This opened the Panorama Merge Preview dialog. Here, I selected the Perspective projection method. I selected this one because I wanted to ensure the lines of the buildings were kept perfectly straight. Although the image preview looked rather distorted, I was able to correct this in the following step.

3 In the Lens Corrections panel, I clicked the Manual tab and adjusted the Vertical and Horizontal sliders to align the vertical lines and horizon. This extreme adjustment also required me to adjust the Rotate, Scale, and Aspect sliders. I then applied a Crop Overlay to trim the edges.

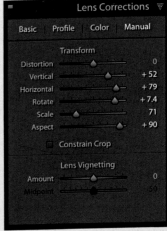

4 in this step, I selected the Graduated Filter tool and added a filter adjustment by clicking near the top and dragging down to the middle of the image. I applied the settings shown here, where I set the Sharpness to -100 and set the Clarity slider to -12. I then added a further Graduated Filter adjustment at the bottom, also applying a negative Sharpness plus Negative Clarity adjustment.

Mask : New **Edit** Brush

Effect :   Custom

Temp		0
Tint		0
Exposure		0.00
Contrast		0
Highlights		0
Shadows		0
Whites		0
Blacks		0
Clarity		− 12
Dehaze		0
Saturation		0
Sharpness		− 100
Noise		0
Moiré		0
Defringe		0
Color		

Reset Close

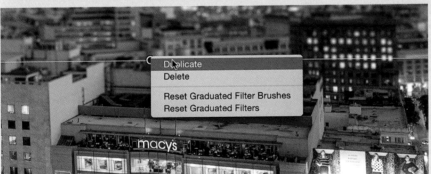

- Duplicate
- Delete

- Reset Graduated Filter Brushes
- Reset Graduated Filters

Basic ▽

Treatment :	Color	Black & White

WB :   As Shot ⇕

Temp	5,750
Tint	+ 6

Tone	Auto
Exposure	+ 0.90
Contrast	− 11

Highlights	− 47
Shadows	+ 96
Whites	− 32
Blacks	− 17

Presence

Clarity	+ 13
Vibrance	0
Saturation	0

5 To strengthen the top blur effect, I clicked to select the pin and right-clicked to reveal the contextual menu shown here, where I selected Duplicate. This duplicated the blur adjustment. I then repeated this step at the bottom. Note there is a limit to how many times you can duplicate a blur adjustment and increase the intensity of the blur. As you add successive negative sharpness adjustments, the blurring effect becomes less pronounced. Finally, I revisited the Basic panel and modified the settings to produce a lighter-looking image.

INDEX